Praise for The Cunni[ng]

"A rich personal medley of folk ma[gic], [with] a strong practical element ideally suited to the newcomer a[nd the] practitioner."
—RONALD HUTTON, professor, historian, and author of *The Witch*

"A hands-on approach to paving a path that is rooted in an endless conversation between the practitioner and their land. Packed to the brim with exercises, charms, spells, and rites, this is a book which provides a firm foundation followed by a true grimoire of operative magic. Beginner and seasoned practitioners alike will be able to draw inspiration from this bubbling cauldron of wisdom."
—MHARA STARLING, author of *Welsh Witchcraft*

"With compassion and expertise, Collins transforms trauma recovery from an overwhelming challenge into an achievable, empowering journey."
—DAWN EIDELMAN, PhD, executive director of the Association for Comprehensive Energy Psychology, executive coach, and award-winning education entrepreneur

"A wealth of information for aspiring witches and cunning folk…Older magical knowledge is carefully balanced with the needs of the modern world and the author's own experience. The book is clearly written from the heart in an accessible style, giving it a genuinely authentic feel. It is sound, practical, joyful, and inspiring."
—VAL THOMAS, author of *Hallowtide* and *Chalk and Flint*

"Forest introduces you to the corners where spirits and familiars congregate, the spaces of power, the super in the natural, and equips you to engage in time-honored magic. As you align better with the energies of the normal and the fantastic, Forest outlines practices that integrate well with each other and suit any number of lifestyles."
—BEN STIMPSON, author of *Ancestral Whispers*

"An erudite, endlessly fascinating, and practical book that will be a welcome addition to any witch's shelf. Filled with knowledge, wisdom, and techniques, this is a book that the working witch will savour!"
—IAN CHAMBERS, author of *The Witch Compass*

"An absolute treasure trove of folk magic and one that will delight you with every turn of the page. Make yourself a cuppa and pull up a chair—the magic is about to begin."
—RACHEL PATTERSON, author of *A Witch for Every Season*

"At once enchanting, comforting, practical, and inclusive, Forest has written a rare gem rooted in lived experience in the landscape of Celtic folk magic. Her impeccable scholarship shines through on every page, indelibly woven with her signature poetic writing style."
—DANIELLE BLACKWOOD, author of *The Twelve Faces of the Goddess*

"In this book, we are given old world magick that can be used for the modern witch. From the moment you turn the page you are transported to the witch's cottage and discover spells, recipes, potions, and the many spirits who fill the home with warmths and power."
—CHRIS ALLAUN, author of *Whispers from the Coven*

"Forest has packed an incredibly detailed treasure of knowledge about the ways of the cunning men and wise women of the British Isles into this book. Yet amazingly, she does so without being prescriptive. She presents you with the choice of following this ancient path verbatim or creating your own personal magical practice. Either way, I can guarantee that you will take this book into your hands time and again."
—CHRISTIAN BRUNNER, author of *Alpine Witchery*

"A comprehensive compendium, clearly drawn from years of personal practice, curious inquiry, and scholarship. Danu herself is a wise cunning woman, guiding us in the ways that have sprung from the land for thousands of years… Not only is one left with a veritable wealth of accessible practices, but there is also a deep connection to where these practices come from."
—TIFFANY LAZIC, author of *Psychopomps & the Soul*

The Cunning Folk's Book of COTTAGE WITCHCRAFT

About the Author

Danu Forest is a traditional Celtic wisewoman who is both British and Irish. She has studied Celtic magic and cunning craft for more than thirty years and is noted for her gift as a natural hereditary seer and her scholarly research. She lives in the wild marshes surrounding the legendary Glastonbury Tor in the southwest of England and is the author of several books, including *Wild Magic: Celtic Folk Traditions for the Solitary Practitioner*, and *Celtic Tree Magic: Ogham Lore and Druid Mysteries*. She holds an MA in Celtic Studies specialising in Fairy lore and the Otherworld.

The Cunning Folk's Book of Cottage Witchcraft

Spells • Charms & Traditions of WILD FOLK MAGIC

Danu Forest

LLEWELLYN
WOODBURY, MINNESOTA

The Cunning Folk's Book of Cottage Witchcraft: Spells, Charms & Traditions of Wild Folk Magic Copyright © 2025 by Danu Forest. All rights reserved. No part of this book may be used or reproduced in any manner whatsoever, including internet usage, without written permission from Llewellyn Worldwide Ltd., except in the case of brief quotations embodied in critical articles and reviews. No part of this book may be used or reproduced in any manner for the purpose of training artificial intelligence technologies or systems.

First Edition
First Printing, 2025

Book design by Rordan Brasington
Cover design by Shira Atakpu
Editing by Laura Kurtz
Interior illustrations on pages 26, 45, 74, 100, 114, 128, 139, 173, 183, 193, 198, 212
    by Dan Goodfellow
Interior illustrations on pages 119–121, 224–226 by Llewellyn Art Department

Llewellyn Publications is a registered trademark of Llewellyn Worldwide Ltd.

Library of Congress Cataloging-in-Publication Data (Pending)
ISBN: 978-0-7387-7747-4

Llewellyn Worldwide Ltd. does not participate in, endorse, or have any authority or responsibility concerning private business transactions between our authors and the public.

All mail addressed to the author is forwarded but the publisher cannot, unless specifically instructed by the author, give out an address or phone number.

Any internet references contained in this work are current at publication time, but the publisher cannot guarantee that a specific location will continue to be maintained. Please refer to the publisher's website for links to authors' websites and other sources.

Llewellyn Publications
A Division of Llewellyn Worldwide Ltd.
2143 Wooddale Drive
Woodbury, MN 55125-2989
www.llewellyn.com

Printed in the United States of America

Other Books by Danu Forest

Wild Magic: Celtic Folk Traditions for the Solitary Practitioner (Llewellyn)

Celtic Tree Magic: Ogham Lore and Druid Tree Mysteries (Llewellyn)

Celtic Goddesses, Witches, and Queens Oracle Deck (Schiffer)

The Magical Year: Seasonal Celebrations to Honor Nature's Ever-Turning Wheel (Watkins)

Cerridwen: Keeper of the Cauldron (Moon Books)

Gwyn ap Nudd: Wild God of Faerie, Guardian of Annwfn (Moon Books)

For the followers of the old ways

Acknowledgments

I would like to thank my family and fellow magical folk for all their support and inspiration over the years, and of course the wonderful team at Llewellyn, especially Elysia Gallo, Laura Kurtz, and the designers for making this book come to life. Finally I would like to thank the spirits of the hearth and heath for their good company and wise counsel.

—Danu Forest, Somerset, 2025

Contents

Practica xiii
Common Sense Disclaimer xvii
Introduction 1

Part One
The Cunning Path:
Conjuring, Charming, and the Way of the Wise Woman

Chapter 1: *The Witch's Cottage* 15
Chapter 2: *Gathering Magic* 31
Chapter 3: *Magical Tools* 51
Chapter 4: *Divination and the Arte of Finding* 63
Chapter 5: *Apotropaic Magic: Household Protections and Wards* 81
Chapter 6: *A Witch's Wheel of the Seasons* 107
Chapter 7: *Moon Magic* 117
Chapter 8: *Wortcunning* 131
Chapter 9: *Familiars and Other Spirits* 155

Part Two
A Cottage Grimoire:
Spells and Charms for Cunning Folk and Wild Witches

Chapter 10: *Candle Spells* 177
Chapter 11: *Healing Spells* 185
Chapter 12: *Love Spells* 197
Chapter 13: *Potions and Powders* 203

Conclusion 221
Appendix: Planetary Virtues, Sigils, and Other Symbols 223
Bibliography 229
Index 233

Practica

Finding the Heart of the Home   20
Vision Journey to Meet the Household Spirits   22
A Hearth Blessing: Smooring the Fire   26
A Spell to Honour and Heal Your Ancestors   28
Drawing Up the Earth   33
A Witch's Walk Through the Forest   34
Using a Staff to Gather Serpent Currents   39
Meeting the Four Airts at the Crossroads   46
Preparing Your Staff or Stang   52
Tuning In to a Tree Spirit   53
Decorating and Preparing Your Wood   55
Seasoning Your Iron Cauldron   57
Scrying with Wild Water   65
Water Scrying at Home   65
Moon Scrying   67
Scrying with a Shewstone   69
Spirit Flight to Seek a Scrying Spirit Ally   70
Fire Scrying   71
Candle Scrying   72
Sieve and Shears   73
Book and Key   74
Tea Leaf Reading   75
Iron Water   83
A Simple Clearing: Sweeping and Salt   84
A Candle Hex Breaker   85
Cord-Cutting Spell to Sever Energetic Bindings   86
Cord-Cutting to Sever Spirit Attachment   88
Three Sticks Method   88
For Resolving Neighbourly Disputes   89

A Ritual House Cleansing with Smoke   91

Hag Stone Charm   94

Rowan and Red Thread   95

Saining Charm for Protection   96

A Charm to Banish the Evil Eye Set upon Someone   97

A Written Protection Spell for the Home   100

Garlic Charm   101

Ash Leaf Wreath   101

Ash Stick Guardian   102

A Simple Modern Witch Bottle Formula   104

Other Witch Bottle Formulas   105

Finding the Flow   119

Moon Water   121

Moon Meditation   122

Spirit Flight: Meeting the Moon   124

Dream Magic   126

Dream Charm Bag   126

Queen of the Night: A Chant in Honour of the Moon   128

A New Moon Lunar Protection Charm   129

Connecting with the Spirits of the Garden   133

Vision Journey to Connect with Plant Spirits   135

A Charm for Gathering Herbs with Magical Purposes   147

To Make a Flower Essence   149

Ice and Snow Spell for Transformation   152

Creating a Thought-Form   159

Gaining an Animal Spirit Familiar   162

Making a Fairy Ally   167

Spirit Flight: Meeting the Fairy King and Queen   169

Meeting the Honoured Dead   172

A Candle for the Spirits   178

A Candle Spell for Prosperity   180

A Candle Spell for Banishing   181
Rolled Wax Love Candle Spell   181
Hag Torches   182
To Cure Warts   185
A Banishing Bag   186
To Stop Nightmares   186
Shoe Spell for Protection   187
Shoe Cure for Nightmares   187
Footprint Banishing Spell   187
Shoe Spell for Prosperity   187
A Sciatica Charm   188
Black Thread Healing Charm for Small Children   188
To Cure a Sore Throat   189
To Cure Sprains and Broken Bones   190
Against Fatigue When Walking   190
Against Weakness of the Eyes   190
To Ensure Good Sight   191
Against Numbness in a Limb   191
Cure to Heal Fairy Darts or Elfshot   192
Healing Withy Cage   192
Protection for Babies and Children   194
To Heal a Burn   194
Healing Witch's Ladder   195
To Regain a Lover   197
Valerian Love Sachet   198
Flowerpot Spell   199
To Keep Love's Bonds True and Strong   199
To Enchant Another to Lust   199
Yarrow Spell   200
To See One's Future True Love by the Moon   201
A Winter Blessing Simmer Pot   204

A House-Cleansing Simmer Pot   204

An Illness-Beating Simmer Pot   205

A Calming and Dreaming Simmer Pot   206

Love Potion Simmer Pot   206

Prosperity Simmer Pot   207

Space-Clearing Protection Spray   208

Comfort and Blessing Spray   209

To See Spirits   210

Mugwort Tisane   210

Mugwort Oil   211

Elderflower Tisane   211

Ancestral Honouring Oil   211

Boundary Wash Recipe   213

Banishing Powder   214

Black Salt   215

Dragon Boundary Protector   216

Rosemary Water   216

Juniper Bundle   217

Protection Incense   218

Blessing Incense   218

Offering Incense   219

Common Sense Disclaimer

The first thing we all need for our magic to be effective is to be empowered. Empowerment comes as a result of discipline, responsibility, and common sense. If you go out into nature, always consider your environment—that is, your practical needs for your safety and well-being as well as the ethical needs of what you are doing. Walk with gratitude, don't take too much from the land, and when you forage (for example), be sure that you can correctly identify everything you touch. Don't put yourself or anyone else in dangerous situations. A certain amount of what you do will always involve risk, but be realistic and take sensible precautions in whatever form they may take. Don't let anything in this book or anywhere else guide you from what you know to be sensible for your own self-care or the safety of others.

With regards to the healing spells and potions found here—you are advised to still seek medical advice where relevant, especially for serious issues, injuries, and the care of children and the infirm. Always consider the practicalities and ethics in what you do and say, especially in prayers and spells.

We also talk about fire and candles in these pages—again, be sensible and safe. Don't set yourself or anything else you don't intend to on fire! Common sense and fire safety are essential for effective magic.

This book also mentions using spring and well water. Again, don't presume water from any outdoor or natural setting is safe to drink—if you aren't sure, there are tests you can buy as well as very effective filters. Be sensible about the context and circumstances you are in, and don't ever ingest anything or give anything to anyone else that you are not 100 percent sure of.

Finally—let your magic be an adventure and an inspiration, not a cautionary tale to others. Be wise, always.

Introduction

I live in an old land, a place where people have lived for thousands of years. My home is a little cottage in Somerset, in the southwest of England, tucked amidst a vast landscape of marshes and secretive hillsides, rivers, and old, ancient woodlands. A few miles from the sea and just a couple of miles from the mystical Isle of Avalon, here the wheel of the seasons turns by the signs of the natural world—herons and otters, the starlings returning in the autumn evenings. The blossom on the cherry plum and the blackthorn are the first signs of spring, the cuckoo calling in summer, the mist at dawn in summer and then at dusk as autumn comes in again, carried on the scents of the land—woodsmoke, ripe apples, and autumn leaves. It's a land of liminal places, where traces of the old ways linger on; humps of Celtic Iron Age roundhouses can be spotted along the fields where brown cows doze and the circular mounds of Bronze Age burial cairns marking the resting places of chieftains decorate the hilltops like strings of beads. Knowledge and people used to come here from the sea rather than across the land, and while the coast could be travelled with ease, the danger was in going inland. The roots and the memory of the land and its people remain deep and still in the black-brown peat, rarely stirring.

The history of magic in a place like this has many faces and phases. Six thousand years ago, the marshes were a place of the spirits; neither land nor earth, they were given gifts of beautiful stone axe heads to appease and honour them. Later when the Celtic tribes lived in roundhouses on stilts above the waters, they honoured the many gods of the land, sea, and sky. Later still came the folk healers, wise women, cunning folk, and conjurers, who spoke to the same spirits on the same hills, saw them in the same dark waters, and healed and helped the same troubles of the people here, one foot in this world and one foot in the other. They treated illness and cast protections on the children, blessed the harvests and the butter churn, spoke to the storms and the wild fairy spirits, and eased the fears of the village when the eerie and uncanny touched their lives.

This old land has seen many of these folk, generation after generation adapting old magics and creating new ones, remembering the old stories and gathering their medicine chests from the hedgerow and the wood. These days we share the land with Christian mystics and New Age healers and everything in between, but the spirits remain, and so do we.

Celtic folk magic and its associated practices have been my lifelong companions. I have practiced magic now for more than thirty-five years and seen spirits my whole life. The how, what, and why of the way I have honed my craft has changed and evolved over that time, adding more knowledge here, more experience there, fine-tuning my intuition and skill along the long road of my life, but one thing has remained since the beginning, a constant: My relationship with the land and the service to its people and all living things. In that way, I am the same as those who have gone before me and those who will surely come after. The land lives, grows trees to clothe it, and conjurers and wise folk to talk with it, as surely as spring follows winter.

My magic and spirituality are based on this endless conversation with the land. I learn its ways from time spent with it in the wild, learning its traditions and tales, dreaming with it over the winter by my hearth fire, and roaming its secret places under summer skies filled with stars.

Folk magic isn't about a formal way—it's not about covens and secret initiations. Instead, it's about growing what we do organically in relation to the land upon which we live and the ancestors in our blood. Like the land, what we do and who we are is made up of many layers and drawn from all the things that come to the land and spring from it. On the British mainland, four nations exist in a small island space no more than a few hours' drive from one corner to the other, making each area distinct in its identity and history but also closely entwined with all the others. The result is a spider's web of practices and traditions that are all interrelated, mirroring both our uniqueness and our similarities. We also have a long history of invasions and cultural shifts that bring new things in from outside. We have Celtic, Roman, Saxon, Norse, and Norman influences together with medieval European and now even American and other modern multicultural layers from around the world—Africa, India, China, everywhere—present in some of our magical traditions. We also of course have our closeness to my beloved Ireland with its own layers of history and lore, in addition to those found in the Isle of Man, the Hebrides, and further out—Shetland and Orkney. What all this means is that my folk magic will be different to your folk magic and everyone else's, as each of us naturally resonates with where we live, where we are from, and what our bones tell us.

My spirit soars and my magic is strongest on the lands that I love, here in the southwest of England and also in Ireland. I am half Irish, so my practice is also strongly based on my Irish heritage and the magic and spirituality of that land, which I also call home. As well as my beloved Ireland, I also have close ties to Wales and Scotland, places I both know very well. I have some very close ties in the Highlands and islands of Scotland and spend a lot of time there. The Welsh border is about forty-five minutes away from where I live, so it's not far, and as a University of Wales alumnus I have a strong relationship with its landscape, culture, and traditions. One of my proudest moments was when the chancellor of my university told us at my MA graduation ceremony to go forth as ambassadors for Wales, as her children. Much of the folklore and practices in the southwest of England are entwined with their close cousins in Wales, just as those in Ireland are close to those found in Scotland. How all these aspects interact in my craft is my own unique blend, organically and intuitively working together moment to moment, year by year, just as yours will be. And although I like to work with my ancestral spirits, I want to make it clear that this practice is open to all and finds unique expression in everyone who uses it, regardless of where they live or what their heritage may be. I encourage you to integrate it respectfully with the lands where you are and your own ancestral spirits. What are commonly thought of as "Celtic traditions" call to many all around the world, and this soul calling (as I term it) is fully valid—hospitality was a cornerstone of ancient Celtic cultures, so if this path calls to you, please know you are welcome here! Above all, be mindful to honour all the traditions, aspects, and ingredients of your practice and make your own individual thread in the great weave of this work one enriched with honour and integrity, with respect and in service to all.

In addition to the land, I am also a lover of books and written knowledge. I love to seek old spells and ancient customs; to that end, I have taken my magical practice to university in Wales and completed an MA in Celtic studies, and now (at the time of writing) am studying for a PhD. My studies are interwoven with everything else I do—as I dive deeper into this ancestral knowledge, I feel myself growing deeper roots, healing and decolonising my ancestral lines, and retrieving knowledge that was lost. Some of this knowledge I am ready to present to you here as a reclaiming of the old ways and our wild spirituality and wild magic so that you, too, may be a wild folk witch, if that is your calling.

What Is Wild Witchcraft and Folk Magic?

As opposed to the high magic of the learned upper classes of the past (particularly in northern Europe), wild witchcraft or folk magic—the magic of the common people—has always existed alongside Christianity and Catholicism, perhaps as part of the long evolution of beliefs related to the local spirits of the landscape, its mythology, folklore, and traditions that existed long ago in the pre-Christian past. Nothing stays locked in a vacuum, especially magic and spirit work, and this form of practice evolves and changes from century to century and person to person, weaving in cultural and historical shifts generation after generation. It is closely entwined with what is called *An Creideamh Sí* ("the fairy faith") in Ireland, a collection of practices with different but equivalent counterparts in Britain that are all to do with relations with the spirit realm and what are known in Britain as the Fairies and the Sidhe in Ireland. These are the native spirits found in the landscape, long feared and yet the focus on wonder and power, found in our folklore and superstitions.

Wise women, cunning folk, and other practitioners in Britain and Ireland often consulted with fairies for their magical powers and knowledge.

Examples abound in Ireland and in Scotland, where numerous testimonies are found in the materials related to the Scottish witch trials. Wales and England also have a long history of fairy folklore and cunning folk. However, in Britain we also have plenty of European magical influences. Historically, angels and demons were also frequently consulted, especially using knowledge drawn from numerous medieval European grimoires. I favour working with the spirits of these lands; you will find very few angels and demons here, which is just my preference. I encourage you instead to contact not only the spirits that come to you but the spirits of the area where you live, including any fairies you may find resident, cautiously, mindfully and respectfully. As already stated, this practice is not closed to anyone of any descent or location, and how we blend the elements of our practice will be a very personal and unique thing. We all have our own roots and spirit connections as well as our preferences and sense of calling, which may be drawn from far and wide. If we integrate these into our magic with awareness and integrity, they can help us grow deeper and stronger, each in our own way.

Cunning men and women are still found across the British Isles to this day, and go by many names: wise women, folk witches; *Pellars* (a hex breaker, from the word "expel") is a popular term found in Cornwall and in much of the southwest, as is the term "conjurer," which has been popular for centuries, referring to someone who conjures spirits. There are also charmers—people who perform healing charms, and in Ireland we find the *Bean Feasa* ("wise woman") and fairy doctors, they who consult with fairies and ease relations between them and humans. A popular term in Wales is a *Swynwraig*, a charmer or witch. The term "witch" itself of course has a long history, and its meaning has changed somewhat, especially since the twentieth century. In centuries past, "witch" was used specifically to mean someone who engaged in malicious magic (*maleficium*), which was usually decided by the courts with terrible consequences. Cunning folk, healers, herbalists, and midwives were all at risk of being considered a witch as were other members of the general public—as such, it was not a term chosen by magical practitioners at the time. It is only recently that it has been claimed and repurposed.

A wild witch or a folk witch is someone who uses and adapts folk magic, and could go by any of the names above depending on their unique perspective. They tend to work closely with nature without attaching themselves to a coven or an initiatory tradition, although traces of these lineages can sometimes be found bound up with certain practices. Folk magic is made of many cultural and historical layers, with few clearly defined lines. Instead, we see a spider's web of interconnected beliefs based on local lore and individual spirit connection and ancestry—of blood or place, or even spirit, stretching across Britain and Ireland, reflecting their own unique identities and their similarities as well as the successive layers of invasion and cultural change. For this reason, everyone's practice will vary from another's and be highly personalised, even if there is extensive common ground and importance placed on local lore and environmental features and resources.

As you read and work with this book, I encourage you to take it as a friend and guide or a sturdy staff to support you in walking your own path, one that connects to your own homes and landscapes as well as your own bloodlines and ancestor spirits in whatever form they take, letting them all inform your practice just as I do with mine. Let this book serve as a rounded primer that supports and inspires you but never constrains your spirit, your magic, or anything you do. That means that your magic may be different to mine—and that's fine. There is room enough for all by the hearth, and we are all still warmed by the same fire. For this reason, I have divided this book into two parts. Part 1, "The Cunning Path," will guide you through the main ideas and practices of our craft, how they have often been applied, and how you can use them as a foundation for your own work. Part 2, "A Cottage Grimoire," is a collection of mostly traditional spells, charms and magical lore, including the recipes for various potions, powders, and incenses that may be of use to you to dip into and apply as needed or as a basis for your own spells and workings and magical creations.

Cottage Craft

The central focus in this book is on folk magic performed largely in and around the cottage as the hub of the wild witch's life. Historically of course, most wise women and cunning folk were from the poorer elements of society, not the magic of stately manors or temples public and private. Instead, this kind of magic is performed in the garden, by the hearth, and on the kitchen table, often in rural locations. Don't let that stop you if you don't live in such a place, however. This book and this magic are still for you. You can still follow and explore the contents in a flat in a city or in a busy family home—you will still have access to whatever you need, living as we do in the modern era, and you are still able to access the land if you try. No matter where you are, spirits of the land, the home, the family still exist, never more than a hair's breadth away. Feel free to adapt and let your approach be organic in how you practice and follow any instructions as guidelines to use with common sense with rather than fixed rules.

Spirits and Fairies and Gods

Throughout this book, we cover working with spirits and fairies, which underpins much of what we do. This sort of cooperation is neither something to take lightly nor something to fear unduly any more than you would encountering other human beings. Imagine meeting a stranger—you are likely to be a mixture of polite, friendly, and reserved with them, cautious and opting to take your time to get to know them before you trust them. Be the same way with the spirits. Fairies and spirits generally are neither inherently good or bad. And while fairies have long been feared by most, they have always our native magical practitioners worked with them and for good reason. Always listen to your gut instincts when working with any of these beings and be sure do your homework. If you are contacting the spirit of a place, check out its folklore and the lore of any previous inhabitants or people there first if you can, as an act of respect and to glean what others may have experienced. Also take your time and heed what your instincts tell you. If you call upon the support of a god or goddess (or a saint for that matter, though you will find very few Christian elements here as that's not my preferred way with one exception to follow), again, do your homework and look into who this being is and what they are about. The matter of whom to contact is a subject too vast to explore here and ultimately everyone will feel differently about who they feel they want to work with, so draw on the many resources out there when available to inform your practice. Let your research be a melting pot of influences, no one being more important than another.

Note that although I do refer to working with Brigit as she is one of my patrons, she has a long history of propitiation in folk magic as a saint and a goddess, especially in Ireland. My work with Brigit draws on my ancestral connection with her. However, Brigit is beloved all across the world; no matter where you find yourself, you are in safe hands with her, so let this be a starting point for you if you are new to this work.

If in doubt, walk softly on this path, be polite, and carry some iron in your pocket as a talisman to keep you safe.

Spirit Flight and Journeying

In this book you will find numerous references and exercises utilising inner vision and meditation or the slightly deeper workings I call "spirit flight." Wise women, cunning folk, and seers have always used their inner vision or second sight to access the spirit realm. The practice can be deeply ritualistic or as simple as tuning in while in a mediative state of mind and hearing your inner wisdom. Sometimes we use guided visualisation techniques to provide handrails for this practice that help steer a practitioner towards connecting with a certain place or spirit or achieving a specific aim. The mind and our imagination function as a powerful translation device in this work and have long been used to help activate and deepen our inner vision and seership capabilities. In this way, we can visualise certain things that represent and function as energetic keys to their presence in the spirit world, and this acts as our internal navigation device to pursue the connections and answers we seek.

The best way to do this work is to be calm and fully present whilst in a gentle meditative or trance state. Don't be intimidated as this is the kind of state of mind we all enter into almost daily at various times; looking out the window on a long journey, or letting your eyes rest on the flames of an open fire, for example, brings these consciousness shifts about. They help us tune out of the daily world a little and make us more able to tune in to other aspects of our awareness.

Some practitioners like to do this work in silence, while others like to use drum beats to assist in this work and that's fine if you feel it helps. Drumming for yourself perhaps with a frame drum or as I do with an Irish bodhrán may take practice but is very effective. However, there are just as many drumming or nature soundtracks available online. If you can avoid it, I don't advise having electrical devices close to you when doing spirit work, but playing something in earshot from a short distance is fine if it works for you.

This practice is perfectly safe, but if you are ever uncomfortable, you don't have to continue and can stop the exercise and return another day (or not) as you wish. Retracing the steps taken in sequence is a good method to easily return consciousness to everyday awareness, helped by eating and drinking and being aware of our bodies to get us grounded again. It's also a good idea to record your experiences in a journal or notebook, as this will often provide insights you weren't aware of at first and can help you spot patterns and flows of information in a way not immediately discernible immediately after a journey.

Practica

Throughout this book you will come across practica (sing. *praticum*): practical exercises, spells, and other practical tasks. These all come from my personal experience and from others, often with centuries of history behind them. However, that doesn't mean that they are written in stone—far from it! They have cultural roots that are important to acknowledge and respect, just as they have been made by people for others to use. So, when you prepare to do some practical work with this book, allow yourself to come to the task in a very grounded and commonsense way. Adapt the words and the techniques to suit your own circumstances, context, and abilities—something that particularly goes for any verbal spells. Let the words you use reflect you and your intentions. For this reason, any words for spells are for guidance only, just to get you going. They will serve perfectly well for the task, and do think carefully about any changes you make but if you feel you want to add to them or adjust them so that they represent you and your aims better, do it! There is no power in feeling you must be someone else in this work; make it your own, and come as you are.

Journalling

Keeping a journal or diary for your magical and spiritual workings is very useful—it helps you reflect upon what you are doing to help you gain insights and spot patterns, just as it helps you notice messages from spirit that may have been missed at the time. It's a very good discipline to get into, and throughout this book after practicum exercises, you may find me suggesting you make notes on what you experienced in your journal. While none of this is compulsory, I do invite you to make as many notes and journal entries as you can when working through these materials, both where I suggest and anywhere else that feels appropriate, as it will aid your progress exponentially.

Common Sense Safety and Disclaimer

Throughout this book you'll be encouraged to go out into nature, sometimes alone, to perform vigils or rituals or just to tune in and draw energy from the serpent currents of the land, as well as to forage and make allies with the living and spirit presences around you. Be sensible when you do these practices—being out in nature, especially alone, will always have risks that require your caution and sensibility. Know your terrain, take note of weather conditions, and make sure you have all the appropriate equipment you may need: water, sunscreen, and minimal survival equipment in addition to the magical items that may be required. If you live in a very hot, cold, or other extreme environment such as where dangerous animals may live, take other sensible safety measures as well. Also be especially cautious if you are a potentially vulnerable person—don't announce that you are going out alone to strangers on social media, for example. Make sure your phone is fully charged. Let trusted people know where you are going and when to expect you back. Your safety is always your responsibility; don't let anything in this book or anywhere else guide you away from what you know to be a good idea for your own self-care.

This book also contains information on using herbs and foraging as well as healing spells. Again, use your common sense here. While they are often very helpful and effective, no herbal folk remedy or spell is a substitute for proper professional medical advice and attention, especially when dealing with more significant or serious conditions or caring for others. Equally, if you have any allergies or underlying health conditions, make sure for yourself that any plants you touch or ingest are safe for you and your specific condition—the same goes for anyone you share these with. Correct identification is also vitally important. Always make sure that you are using the plant you think you are. There are tons of resources out there that help with identification, and every plant mentioned in this book includes its Latin name to assist you in correct, accurate identification. Don't skip this even if you are confident with your herbs; double-check because the price of making a mistake can be high. When it comes to foraging, always be mindful when taking anything from nature: Don't take too much, and never the last of anything. Always make sure you have permission to forage from the landowner if relevant, and leave plenty for nature, the birds, bees, and other creatures who may rely on the plant as a food source. Also be aware of pesticides and other chemicals that may be used on plants on roadsides and other areas.

Finally, there is a lot of talk in this book about visiting holy wells and using spring water. Again, use common sense—you are responsible for your own safety. Don't presume water from a fresh spring is safe to drink. If in doubt, there are tests you can buy as well as very effective filters. Be sensible about the context and circumstances you are in, and don't ever ingest anything or give anything to anyone else that you are not 100 percent sure of.

And Finally...

Remember to enjoy this as a very special spiritual path. Enjoy your magic. Let it infuse your day and touch the threads of your life with its special moonlit fingers, dusting the mundane with its moth dust and fairy dew, that certain, secret thing that adds a bit of wonder and adventure to life. All of us who are animists, spirit workers, and magic practitioners in any form are by our natures adventurers who love the mystery, the touch of the unknown and unseen in this life. We strain at the edge of the fields we know as we listen for the song of the stars. Let that sense be the thing that keeps the fire in your heart and the sparkle in your eye—protect it against sun and storm for the treasure it is.

Part One

The Cunning Path

*Conjuring, Charming,
and the Way of the Wise woman*

Here we will explore the fundamental grounding ideas and practices of our venerable craft: the hows and whys and the application of these in our daily practice around or near the home. The home is, after all, however it is formed, our sanctuary and seat of sovereignty within ourselves, the place of our power as well as our rest. The hub of this work is by necessity local and focused on where we spend most of our time and the magic we may perform at our hearth sides and houses. We will explore here the different aspects of spirit work and spirit flight, protection and sacred space, scrying and finding, working by the moon and the seasons, and the tools, herbs, and other natural materials we may work with—all with a focus on how we apply them to our lives and daily practice and how we may use them to help others. Most of what you will find here is traditional knowledge and lore to which I have added my own insights and how I have used these things in my own practice. There are no hard and fast rules; each of us inherits this magic to use as we feel we should. To sit in the place of our power and be effective with this craft is to do two things: on one hand, acknowledge and honour the roots and ancestries of our practice; on the other, wield that magic and weave a future thread according to our needs and the needs of those around us, adding to its rich tapestry one generation after another.

Chapter 1
The Witch's Cottage

In this chapter we look at the importance of the hearth and home as spirit beings in their own right and explore how we can work with that to the best effect. Where we live, where we rest, eat, love, and connect with others is the centre of our magical compass in the outer world, just as our heart is the centre of our inner world. Whether a cottage, a house, a flat in a high-rise or a live-in van, our homes are our fortress and sanctuary, the centre of our work and the storehouse and engine room of our power.

Folk Magic Around the Home

There are a host of ways we can apply folk magic to our homes, protecting, blessing, and adding a magical and spiritual element to our daily lives and our sacred living space. To the cunning folk and wise women, magic is not separate from everyday life—it is woven through it, making a rich and vibrant tapestry both meaningful and utterly practical. And magic itself is not a separate thing; it is positioned centrally in the practitioner's life and mindset, so there is no boundary between our understanding of energy and the spirit world and the grounded details of life. They are one and the same.

Here are a few ways in which we can apply folk magic to each room in our home. Don't worry too much about the detail at this stage; the following pages will give you all the skills you need to apply these ideas to your home in ways that works for you.

Front Door and Hallway

The front door (and the back door if you have one) is a key boundary area where spirits welcome or unwelcome may make ingress into your space. Doorways and other liminal spaces may function as practical physical doorways and also as entry points from the spirit realm, serving as the nexus points in the space's psychic geography. For this reason, it's important to think of doorways on multiple levels. Make sure the door can securely lock and has a clear entry and exit that is neither blocked nor overly exposed. At the same time, consider it from a metaphorical or magical standpoint. The things you place around a doorway can have added significance to flavour the environment in certain ways. You can place all sorts of protective items in this area, but be sure to get the balance right between boundaries and blessings so that the good stuff is welcomed and the negative is kept at bay.

Doorsteps and under door mats are good places to leave a line or layer of salt, as well as a scatter of protective herbs. These are also good places to put protective sigils to ensure nothing unwelcome may pass through.

Protective staffs or a broom are good things to keep by a door, as are bowls of salt and blessing herbs such as vervain, or rose petals to draw love into your home. An iron item around a doorway is a great idea—the traditional horseshoe is perfect for this. Equally, a hag stone (a stone with a natural hole formed in it) and a key charm (a large iron key charged with guarding the boundaries, locking and unlocking the psychic boundary as required) is a great idea too. Rowan crosses tied with red thread are traditional protective charms placed at doorways and windows that will increase how aware you are of the energies or spirits coming and going, as rowan helps increase pyschic vision. Mirrors can be very useful at doorways, but consider first if they are needed: If you feel your home has too much coming through that you don't want, such as an unfriendly neighbour perhaps, or a churchyard, a mirror can reflect back what we don't want and prevent its entry.

Having a spirit guardian at your doorway is a very powerful way to control what can enter and what must stay outside. These spirits can be invoked by prayer or even given a spirit home of their own such as a little spirit house or you can place the spirit's essence in a guardian statue or garden ornament.

Witch bottles and spirit traps are also useful by the front and back doors if you believe they are needed. Bells, chimes, and bunches of blessing herbs can also be hung around an entry space to keep it energetically clear from more general toxic energy and to draw in good spirits and energies.

The Kitchen

The kitchen is a powerful place in the psychic geography of the home. A larger kitchen that can accommodate people around a table is an important place where relationships are maintained as well as where food is prepared. No matter the kitchen's size, the energy we want in this space is primarily blessing—a small altar to the gods and spirits of the food, of crops and hunting perhaps, as well as to the household spirits to bless our food and support our abundance. A small offering dish somewhere in the kitchen where we share a portion of our meals is a lovely way to make this an everyday thing to remind us of the spirits' presence and keep regular, good relations with them.

You can also place in your kitchen a small shrine or a central candle to light in honour of and blessing your relationships. I have a small centrepiece on my kitchen table where I light a candle and place flowers around it to honour all my relationships—friends and family, work, and of course the spirit realm.

You can also of course infuse your cooking with good magic, and the subject of kitchen witchery is one unto itself. I like to cook in a conscious way that infuses blessings into the food—I say prayers over the food and stir clockwise or deisil to energise what will be eaten.[1] I also use wooden utensils with blessing sigils and symbols on them, especially the Brigit's cross and the sun wheel.

Remember to make use of any windows in the kitchen as well. I use my sunny kitchen windowsill as a key place to hang herbs to dry and to infuse tinctures and elixirs with the sun's power.

Lounge and Hearth

The lounge is often the most communal space in the home and in traditional houses it will often feature a hearth of some form. Like doorways, these are liminal spaces where the spirits may enter via the chimney and thus have always traditionally been places of focused magical protection. Traditional

---
1. Irish Gaelic for sunwise or clockwise, often Anglicised in modern Wicca to *deosil*.

witch bottles have been found buried around the hearths in old houses in the United Kingdom, as have mummified cats, used as protective guardian spirits, and old shoes to draw baneful spirits away from their owners. Horseshoes, rowan crosses, witch marks, and other items and charms have also been found, and all have a long history of use around the hearth. While our modern homes may not necessarily have traditional hearths with chimneys, most still feature an area for lounging where we can find our energy focuses, such as around a gas fire or even around a TV. For this reason, protective charms need to be placed in areas that make sense to the home as it is. We could very well place magical items under the floorboards in our homes, but it may be more sensible to place a witch bottle on a shelf—perhaps hidden in an attractive box by the TV where all sorts of energies may enter our homes rather than by our modern central heating, for example.

Like the kitchen, the lounge is another space where we can honour the household spirits and place offerings to them. The windows and space of the main room of the house are good places to hang spirit houses and witch balls for protection and to honour the unseen residents of our homes. Another option is making a shrine to protect and nurture the family relationships or other social connections. One way to do this that is both simple and attractive is using a large blessed candle surrounded by family photos or small items relating to each family member. The candle can then be lit and prayers made for the well-being of all household members and to strengthen the bonds of love between everyone.

Bedrooms

Bedrooms are places where we want peaceful rest as well as romance. One item that frequently appears in relation to this room are protective charms to help people sleep well and have good dreams. Nightmares may come along in times of stress but can also sometimes indicate the presence of unwelcome spirits or psychic attacks.

Iron, rowan crosses tied with red thread, or a pouch of rowan berries are excellent charms to protect from bad dreams. When combined with mugwort, they add a level of prophecy and psychic awareness to your dreams. Moonstones placed under your pillow or in a dish by the bed grant wise dreams and restful sleep, and charm bags of chamomile and lavender under your pillow will also aid sleep and ease a troubled mind. Children's bedrooms in particular benefit from protective charms; it was common to place rowan crosses and pieces of iron under cribs to protect the child from unwelcome spirits. This practice can be applied to children of all ages, but be mindful to place any items somewhere safe out of the reach of curious children, and don't use anything toxic or irritant or sharp for these spaces. You could also use blessing herbs and plants to create the good atmosphere you want around children: vervain, rose, apple, and chamomile are what I use in conjunction with rowan wood and a small smooth-edged iron horseshoe.

Meadowsweet, mistletoe, and roses are all powerful herbs for love spells and can be hung by the bed to increase a sense of romance in the air. A charm bag of chilli, ginger, and sugar can increase passion. Green or red candles can also be used inscribed with your and your partner's name to add love and sex magic into the space.

Healing herbs can also be placed in charm bags or in bowls to make healing charms in sick rooms or to create a healing supportive atmosphere for the elderly or infirm; although practicality and safety must always come first, combinations of protective healing and blessing ingredients can be powerful allies for supporting those in need without resorting to more direct magical intervention.

Bathrooms

Bathrooms are places in the house that are as sensual as they are practical, for cleansing and cleaning. One way to think about this room in magical terms is to consider it a place to honour the water spirits. A small shrine to the spirits of the rivers and springs can help draw blessings in as well, honouring the water spirits and maintaining a good relationship with them. Any attempts to honour water spirits of course start with practical matters (for example, using ecofriendly cleaning products), but we can also create a shrine in the bathroom with found items such as shells, or set out a bowl of river water and pebbles to create a space for the water spirits in our home that makes us more mindful of their support.

Homemade remedies in the form of herbal charm bags run under the tap at bath time or making our own magical herbal bath milks, oils, and salt scrubs all add extra elements to our cleansing rituals. Charging and blessing our bathwater by adding blessed spring water is also very effective. All these things can be adapted to our needs at the time.

Lofts, Basements, and Other Less Used Spaces

The lesser used parts of a house can easily collect unsettling feelings in our imaginations, but they are also places where spirits, especially ghosts, may hide to keep out of the way of human interactions. Stuck feelings and stagnant energies can also linger in places where there is no regular flow of energy and life, especially if old and unused items are stored there. For this reason, such places should always be included in any house blessing or cleansing work, even if they are physically empty. Incense of other cleansing sacred smoke is very useful in such places, though be mindful that dusty lofts and cobwebs present a fire risk. Equally, the use of water should also be carefully considered, as you don't want to encourage dampness in a space. The best approach is to visit and cleanse the area regularly, and, if possible, open any doors and windows to let the air move and energies flow again. Also be aware of any negative energies attached to any items kept in storage and cleanse them when necessary.

The Heart of the Home

Whatever kind of home you have, it has a central space, the area where most of the energy or activity within the space is centred. For some, it's a kitchen table; for others, it's a fireplace. Where is it in your home?

Practicum
Finding the Heart of the Home

Take a good look around your space to see if you can figure out the energy flow of your home. As you feel into it, remember to use your common sense. Any areas of clutter are likely to be either heavily used or where things and perhaps stagnant energy accumulate and cannot find release and balance. Take time to notice: Does your home feel as if things can't settle? Is it comfortable? Can you relax there?

If you feel there isn't a heart to your space (sometimes modern spaces with open floor plans in particular can feel this way), building an altar can really help. Over time, the whole feel of the space will change and settle. And if your home does have a heart, it will benefit from an altar both to serve as a centre for your magical work and to honour the helpful household spirits residing there.

Household Spirits

Over time, a house or other type of building will develop its own spirit and own identity, as chances are it will live far longer than its various human inhabitants. It seems to me that a household spirit is sometimes a spirit of place, a nature or land spirit who resided on the spot where the building was built; at other times, these spirits are shaped or even made as a result of the energy created in the space. Like us, these spirits change, grow, and evolve over time.

In addition to household spirits that are the spirit of the house or home itself, there are sometimes spirits who reside in the building. People who have passed in the home may sometimes remain in spirit form, and those who have had particularly emotional times there may leave an energetic imprint. Other spirits may also take up residence for a variety of reasons—some of these may be welcome, others not.

Meeting the Household Guardian Spirits

Key to this work is building a relationship with the good and helpful spirits in your locality to such an extent that you build up a team that can work with you to protect your space or periodically assist in your workings. This team can also alert you to trouble, help find lost objects, and generally care for the place. Build these relationships slowly and consistently for the best results, putting in plenty of patience and learning to listen to them so it's not just a one-sided conversation.

Wherever you live, that patch of land will have its resident spirits who have been there always. When your home was built, some spirits may have moved or receded further from human awareness while others may have become part of the spirit landscape of your home. These spirits will affect how your home feels as much as you affect it in addition to whatever practical physical issues the space may have regarding temperature, light, size, airflow, and so on. It's good to build a relationship with the positive spirits of the home and either remove or resolve the issues of any negative spirits or energies there. Note that when I'm talking about spirits, I'm not referring only to ghosts or exclusively those who were once human spirits; I'm including the wider spirit world—nature spirits and spirits of place—who may look human but never were, or were long, long ago but are now something else.

When you have located the heart of your home, try setting up a household altar if you haven't already—a space set aside as near as is practical to that energetic hub of the house solely for honouring the spiritual and magical side of your life where you can acknowledge good and helpful household spirits. Speak aloud who the altar is for and use your own words to make it clear it's for the friendly spirits you would welcome in your home, not anyone else. Do the same every time you place an offering upon it. Sometimes talking aloud like this makes us acknowledge to ourselves that these beings are real and reveal to us what we already knew but hadn't consciously processed regarding what spirits are around us and what they are like. Your conversation doesn't have to be formal—a light conversational tone is fine, so just communicate and let it flow. Feel out what kind of response you are getting and what kind of offering they would like—a common one for me is to make them a cup of tea, but offerings of food and other drink, incense, or flowers are also suitable.

When you have made offerings for a while (a few days or a couple of weeks should be sufficient), seek out the household spirit in your inner vision. It will be easier if you have the second sight, but if not, the exercise is still useful in helping you build your relationship and increase your sensitivity towards who is around in your home and what's going on. It will also become clearer with practice.

Practicum
Vision Journey to Meet the Household Spirits

This exercise can be very simple; unless your home feels like a very negative space, you needn't put up any protection or cast any kind of circle for it—in fact, what you're doing is checking out what's there without any energetic interference of your own, so long as it feels okay to do so.

Go to the heart of the house—the hearthside is ideal if it functions as the heart of your home. Burn some protective or blessing incense, light a candle, and sit quietly, breathing deeply until you feel centred and calm.

Close your eyes, let yourself feel your feet on the ground where you sit, and let the day fall away, focusing your mind on being really present exactly where you are in time and space. In your inner vision, look around the room where you sit: How does it look and feel to you now? Let your inner vision move around the home: How is it different than its every day appearance? You may be surprised at what you learn.

Ask for a guardian spirit of your home to step forward: Do you get a response? The spirit may take any form, so be open to possibilities. Ask that any other spirits in the home reveal themselves and see who else is in your space. It's important to take notice of whomever appears and assess whether they appear sentient—are they aware of you or not? You may notice spirits that appear more like recordings and others that can acknowledge you. See if any guardian spirits who come forth can advise you on what your home needs and what other energies are present. Images, symbols, and feelings that flow as a stream of consciousness are just as useful and communicative as clear dialogue, so be aware you may have to unpack and analyse any messages you receive. Ask the spirits how you can help them and how they can help you. This is your first step towards a positive reciprocal relationship. And although it may take several tries to begin to be fruitful, in time your relationship with your household spirits may be one of your strongest magical resources.

After you feel enough time has passed and the spirits have given you all the information they can, thank them, and let yourself come gradually back into your daily awareness. Open your eyes and breathe deep—feel the breath in your lungs and your feet on the floor. Wiggle your fingers and toes and give yourself a good stretch to come back to your body. Conclude by making the household guardian spirit an offering. If you have received any insights about what needs doing, take tangible practical steps to get that underway.

Offerings and Relating

See if you can get a sense of your household guardian's likes and dislikes to be considerate of their needs. Sometimes your requests may require negotiation and at others, you will need to prioritise your boundaries. But if you can show through your deeds that it is best to live in harmony with them as part of the spiritual ecosystem of the home and its surrounding land, you will find you garner support much quicker than if you seek to be overly dominating. Some boundaries are understood to all—for example, the protection of or noninterference with children is one line all living things know to not cross, and a vast body of magic exists to create and reinforce those boundaries. When it comes to something like cutting down a tree, planting this instead of that, placing a path (or even the house itself) here rather than there, you will often find the household and local spirits have very strong clear wishes that are not hard to accommodate and are often beneficial for all.

In Ireland, traditionally the placement of houses was carefully chosen so as to not offend the Sidhe by making sure they were not built on fairy roads or on a fairy forts, as they are places of power. Equally, certain trees (mostly hawthorns) were and still are never interfered with to ensures right relationship with the spirits of the land and the maintenance of the area's energetic quality. You will find the same applies in large areas everywhere on Earth as well as in microcosm, around the home. Working with this energy and those who maintain it is usually the best way, especially if we want to perform magic at the site.

Another aspect of building this relationship is giving offerings. In Celtic cultures, they were traditionally things like milk or butter, though what you offer depends very much on where you are in the world and what spirits you are dealing with. Equally you may find that if you live somewhere different than where your ancestors lived, the sprits around you may sometimes appreciate a mixture of offerings relevant to both your ancestry and the land where you now live. Sometimes this takes careful thought as not all cultural practices—like traditional offerings—are open to outsiders. Others need to make ethical considerations, such as their environmental footprint or fair-trade practices. With some consideration and respect, it's possible to find a way to honour the land and the ancestral spirits where you live, and indeed making an effort and thinking carefully goes a long way to communicating your wish to build respectful relations.

I like to make butter or bake small cakes for the spirits I work with in addition to bird seed and food for other wildlife as an offering out on the land (as well as part of my responsibility as its guardian). And as previously mentioned, a cup of tea in a special cup is just the thing for ancestral and some household spirits. My offerings are a result of me knowing my land and the spirits who dwell here rather than a fixed thing from a tradition. This personalisation and pragmatism, this balance between lore and lived experience on the ground, are to me what folk magic is about. You can't build relationship with anything or anyone if you feel you already know all you need to know.

Spirit Houses

A spirit house is an excellent way to honour a household's helpful spirits and can be made from almost anything. Rather than entrapping devices known as spirit traps, the spirit house is a place where a welcome and protective spirit may dwell to watch over and protect the home. It is made out of gratitude and appreciation, and it makes a good place to leave offerings for the household spirits.

Some spirit houses look like houses in miniature similar to bird houses and can have objects placed inside them that may honour the spirits while others are carefully made by hand. I greatly enjoy making spirit houses out of willow or hazel, weaving them into spheres I hang in the house or around the property. Each one is a little different and hung with a specific spirit and purpose in mind, but in addition to that personalisation I may often hang a hag stone and herbs within it and perhaps feathers from birds or even bells beneath it. When the spirit house is complete, I take it to where it will be housed and ask the spirit to receive my gift and use it as their home within my home.

In some places where the spirits of the house are not malicious but have felt disrespected and become disruptive, offering them a house has created far more peace and harmony in the atmosphere and has been a significant step into healing the situation. In other circumstances, spirit houses are very powerful tools to assist in working with powerfully protective spirits to see that the home is thoroughly blessed and protected enough to repel strong attacks.

Illustration 1: Spirit House and Hag Stone

Practicum
A Hearth Blessing: Smooring the Fire

If you have a hearth or fireplace of any kind, you may like this protective and blessing prayer to the goddess Brigit when settling the fire for the night. Feel free to adapt it if you don't have live fire, as you wish.

If you have an open fire, gently sperate the embers when it has burnt low into three parts using a poker. Draw a circle with the poker around the embers while visualising that you are casting a compass (that is, encompassing) circle around the home, saying the following:

> *I smoor the fire this night*
> *As Brigit would smoor it,*
> *Brigit's encompassing be on this fire,*
> *Brigit's encompassing be on this household.*
> *May her compassing be about ourselves*
> *May her compassing be about us all,*

May her compassing be about the flock and all animals,
May her compassing be upon this hearth.
Who keeps the watch this night
But Brigit,
The bright and gentle Brigit of the kine.
Whole be house and herd.
Whole be son and daughter.
Whole be wife and husband.
Whole be household all![2]

Ancestor Spirits

Some of the spirits we may encounter around our homes will be ancestors, ours or those connected to the history of the land. Ancestors present us with great opportunities for learning and healing, and we can form powerful allies with some, though not all will be helpful spirits. We may find that some first require our assistance or may even be beings we need to protect ourselves against. The subject of ancestors is a vast category of magic, but we can make our first steps in this area with a few simple things, again revolving around the idea of relationship.

Personal Ancestors

We can rely on our inner knowing to sense if a spirit presence is an ancestor or not, but I encourage you to ground your ability to sense by first familiarising yourself with your family history and tree where possible. If you do this, pay particular attention to the stories your family tells, and keep half an eye on spotting family patterns of behaviour or interest. Some consider all the spirits of your dead relatives going back however far to be your ancestors, but I prefer to narrow that definition down a bit into something more workable. See if you can locate, sense, or call in the presence of helpful ancestors, for example ones who have chosen to guide and support the family or who may have faced problems similar to ones you face currently.

---

2. My adaptation, from Alexander Carmichael, *Carmina Gadelica: Hymns and Incantations* (Floris Books, 1994), 297–98. *Kine* means "cattle."

These ancestors will not be the spirits of recently departed family members—the latter have other things they need to do that usually involves letting go of their lives here. It's more common for them to be spirits of your bloodline who lived long ago *and* specifically chose by their natures to remain supportive of their kin. Although all families have these, most don't have very many, but they will be there and will respond if you call. Equally present are those ancestors who need the help of the living; if we are observant, it's likely we'll spot family patterns that pass on wounds, trauma, and unhealthy behaviours generation after generation. Working to heal these ancestors can close these generational wounds in both directions of the family tree. And as it is with so much of this work, healing ancestral wounds is done through relationship—through acknowledging, remembering, honouring.

Of course, families take on many forms and shapes—some will have blended, adoptive, or other types of structures. And there are also families made of friendships, customs, and shared traditions, for example ancestors on our spiritual path. These types of families are just as valid as ancestors by blood and, in some cases, are even more powerful and influential in our lives than the people to whom we were born. Therefore, working with these ancestors is just as important. The work of honouring and healing them is just as vital to our own well-being and the well-being of those who come after. This work can be done in exactly the same way work with our relations of flesh and blood is done.

Here is a framework for beginning or continuing ancestral work. Adapt it to suit your situation in any way you wish.

Practicum
A Spell to Honour and Heal Your Ancestors

This working can be performed at any time but is most potent at Samhain or a dark moon.

Take two pillar candles and place them side by side on your altar or somewhere suitable—one for your mother's side of your ancestry and one for your father's. Space permitting, you could also place additional candles behind and to the left and right of each candle, to signify their parents and so on—three generations is good but often impractical if you don't have much space. (For those with the least space, a single candle will do.) You can include living family members in your candles if you wish. Remember to adapt and use your intuition as well as your common sense.

Anoint each candle with a little ancestral honouring oil (see recipe page 211) if you wish or inscribe the name of each family member on each candle using a pin.

Settle before the candles, breathing deeply to centre yourself and draw in your focus. My altar is at my hearth so I don't feel the need to cast a circle for this work, but you can if you wish, especially if there are family members in your past or who are deceased that require your caution. If that's the case, draw a circle around the candles themselves with salt.

Take a lit match or taper and light each one in turn stating aloud who it acknowledges. For example:

May this candle honour the bloodline of my mother.
May this candle honour the bloodline of my father.

You could also use the family members' names. If you are working with other kinds of ancestors, state their name and position them however you feel is appropriate. The important thing is that you do this your way.

When each candle is lit, speak to them—tell them the things you remember about them and, if you'd like, anything you now wish to say or wish you had said. Let yourself enter a dialogue with this person for a while. Above all, focus on remembering the ancestor's goodness and viewing their failings with compassion. If difficult feelings arise, give voice to them to release any stuck energy you may be holding—this is healing work, after all—but again, remember to keep in mind the spirit's humanity and fallibility if possible. Dialogue may take several sessions. And if this approach isn't appropriate for you, leave that ancestor for as long as you wish and instead turn your attention instead to a different ancestor or a different aspect of your family patterns and interactions. Ask that a good spirit of that bloodline comes to assist you and for helpful ancestors of that line to support you with this healing. Let the process be an organic one but focus it on honouring and acknowledging both you and them. Sometimes just acknowledging and remembering someone does a great deal to settle their energy as a spirit and can send healing ripples in every direction.

When you feel you have cleared the way if that's what you need to do, speak of the things you are proud of about them, the gifts you have received from them that you value and are grateful for.

You may decide to end the working after a while or pause it to resume another night. If you decide to end the working, conclude by taking a few breaths and bless each side of your bloodline. See it as whole with many individuals within it and give them thanks for bringing you into being as the person you are today. You might like to use these words as an example:

I bless you ancestors of my mother's line and thank you for the gift of life and learning.
I bless you ancestors of my father's line, for all that you have given me!

Let yourself speak from a good place within yourself, expressing your truth as you see it. Know that you are just as powerful as them and you too will contribute to this line going forwards. In time, ideally, anything difficult will have been said, and from there you can do this work purely as an honouring ritual that acknowledges what they have given you with gratitude and peace. With regular practice, you will find ancestral contact around you easier and taking a more positive shape, though don't rush things. Remember, too, that there is no shame in confronting your shadows on this path—that is how we bring change.

If you are lucky enough to have no difficult feelings or family stories to work through, go straight to honouring them: Verbally praise their achievements in life and express your gratitude to them. Honouring them will increase the blessings upon your ancestral lines exponentially and fuel positive energy within you that will bless future generations.

Snuff out each candle if you wish to continue the working another night. Alternatively, when you have blessed each candle and what and who they represent, let them burn down safely.

You could also snuff them now and light them with a simple blessing for a few hours here and there until they are burned down to continue sending your blessings and healing to them over a larger span of time.

Chapter 2
Gathering Magic

The cunning or wise woman's power comes largely from the land. A certain natural aptitude helps a great deal, but the ability to connect with the powerful places of the earth to recharge and align with their energetic flow is something we all can learn. In times of need, illness, or struggle, connection with the land is the cottage witch's main support. The landscape around us houses the main spirits with which we will interact and gain knowledge from, and care of the landscape and the bonds between the human and spirit inhabitants—the good will between these neighbours—is a key if often subtle part of cunning folk practice.

The earth itself is an ever-giving source of magical power, especially if we are wise to its ebbs and flows so that the work we do is in alignment with its current of increase and decrease, inbreath and outbreath over the seasons and the moon's rotations. This is not to say, however, that the earth is the same everywhere in terms of the energy we may find and how accessible it is—there are certain places in the world where far greater amounts of this earth energy (also known as serpent power or serpent currents) can be felt, and within any landscape are places where the energy is richer and more accessible just as there are places where it is more muted and harder to access. This earth energy is not static—it moves in sinuous lines across our earth known in our native Irish and British traditions by numerous names: fairy roads, corpse or coffin roads, dragon or serpent lines, and ley lines. In Cornwall and part of the West Country, the energy itself is called *sprowl*. These avenues of earth energy are places where spirits naturally congregate and flow along, and the manner in which we interact with them can have a profound effect upon us. While a cunning man or wise woman may use these places to draw energy and to work magic, they are not suitable for human habitation; in Ireland there is a strong taboo against building a house or any other structure upon a fairy road, and such places become terrible places to live: The spirits run amok and cause great damage, up to cursing the inhabitants and causing their deaths and those of their families for generations to come.

Magical folk may gather this earth energy in many ways, most often by cultivating a relationship with the land, loving it and knowing it well, and spending time with it in solitude, or by tending to it in a garden or walking its ways through the seasons, rain or shine.[3] There are quite a few landscapes particularly important and beloved to me on these green islands, but the ones with which I have close loving relationships especially—where I have roots along the Boyne Valley in Ireland and my own local landscape where I have lived for many years in the rural South West of England—are as dear to me as any other living being I am close to. I'm aware of them as sentient, intelligent, and deeply feeling beings in their own right. They're beings made of vast swaths of others, to be sure, but they're still unique and living as singular beings.

Some magical practitioners and cunning folk use a staff or walking stick to draw up the land's serpent energy and store it for their magical use later, but it can also quite naturally be drawn up into the body. We breathe it in as air, we absorb it from the earth in the food we eat and the water we drink, and we draw it up through the soles of our feet against the earth. We even draw it in through our hands as we tend to the earth and plants in a garden. We can maximise this quite easily by focusing in on our energy fields and our breath.

---

3. I write more about this in my book *Wild Magic: Celtic Folk Traditions for the Solitary Practitioner* (Llewellyn Publications, 2020).

Practicum
Drawing Up the Earth

Sit on the earth or floor with your legs crossed and your back straight. Breathe deeply and slowly, not in a forced way—let it come gently and feel it in your belly, slowing down to follow the rhythm of your breath. Align your breath with the slow steadiness of the earth beneath you. Let your shoulders drop and send your intention, focusing your inner vision down into the earth directly beneath you. Concentrate on being fully present in where you are in time and space. Feel the earth holding you steady and, using your breath, breathe in the land, up into your body—see it like a slow rising tide of light growing up your feet into your legs, into your abdomen, up your spine, and into your chest. Slowly raise your arms as it rises to your throat, down into your shoulders and arms, and into your hands. Allow yourself to breathe out when you need to, just holding the light steady and feeling that deep connection with the land. And then as you breathe in again and as your arms rise, pull more of the energy up into you and feel it rising into your head. Let the energy keep rising, filling you with light and your whole energy field and the area around you, all anchored and breathing in and out with the earth.

When you want to finish the work, lower your arms and place your palms on the ground to gently disconnect, wiggling your fingers and toes, and thanking the land for its gift.

Woods and Wild Places

If we are fortunate enough to live near or in wilder or more rural areas, we may find we have many of the resources we need spiritually as well as practically in the land around us. This availability is especially evident if we live near woods or forests where we may find herbs and trees we can use in our magic as well as wood for wands and other tools. In addition to this, we have access to the vast gatherings of nature spirits that abound in woods and forests, and the rich, ever-flowing life force that can be tapped into when we walk through a place where nature is the dominant force rather than humanity. As so many folktales around the world will attest, the forest was always understood as a place of spiritual and magical peril since ancient times, but to the practitioner it is where the majority of wilder spirits are found, and it can be a great source of power. Knowing a woodland well means knowing all the forms of life that may be found there. This knowledge is not something that may be learned on one or even several trips—it is the study of several years and seasons, each more enriching and enlightening than the last.

⭒ Practicum
A Witch's Walk Through the Forest

Try this exercise as often as you like to develop your reading of the woods and the types of trees, plants, and wildlife you encounter to develop your sense of the spirits in these places.

Choose a day when you have plenty of time and are alone or in quiet, thoughtful company that will not impede you too much. After a while, you may develop your senses to the point where you can still read the woods in the company of children and other distractions, but try to make time to deepen your abilities and awareness alone whenever you can. There is nothing like meditative time spent communing with the spirits of trees and learning the deep, slow thinking of the forest.

Before you begin, stand at the entrance to the woods or the forest path where you find yourself. In this place be aware that you stand at the edge of different territory, the border of a great collective interconnected community of beings.

When I'm at this place, there is a prayer I like to make; I live just outside Glastonbury in Somerset, which is thought to be one of the realms of the Welsh/Brythonic god Gwyn ap Nudd. You could use this prayer wherever you live or create your own, personalising it using the known or unknown spirits and local gods of your area.

Before speaking, raise your arms and bow your head for a moment. Say aloud:

> *To the king of Spirits, and to his queen—Gwyn ap Nudd, you who are yonder in the forest, for love of your mate, permit us to enter your dwelling.*[4]

---

4. Carl Lindahl et al., *Medieval Folklore: A Guide to Myths, Legends, Beliefs and Customs* (Oxford University Press, 2002), 190. For more information on Gwyn ap Nudd, see my book *Gwyn ap Nudd: Wild God of Faerie* (Moon Books, 2017).

Gwyn ap Nudd is the ruler of the Brythonic otherworld, Annwfn (as it is known in Welsh; Annown in Cornish), and king of the Welsh Fairy spirits the *Tylwyth Teg* ("the fair family"). He is often considered a horned god or a lord of the forest. The prayer that appears here is one medieval Welsh soothsayers recited whenever they entered the forest.

Take time to feel yourself at the beginning of something with the vast hosts of the forest ahead of you, and start walking quietly, listening, as you make your way through the trees. Take note of each tree you pass or as many as you can. Note their species and see if you can identify any of the plants growing around you. Listen and become aware of the wind direction if there is any and note any birdsong: Can you identify which bird it is? And beyond identifying its species, can you see it in the branches or wherever it sits? Can you glimpse its beak open in song? Who could it be communicating with? Does it warn others of your advance? Become aware of the movement of birds around you and the movement of any animals, if you are lucky. In British and Irish woodlands, the animals are most often small and therefore easily overlooked—shrews and mice, maybe squirrels, and if you are very lucky, badgers at dusk, foxes, and even deer. You must walk quietly, with a stilled and calm spirit to see them, as they will see and sense you well before you will spot them usually. If you surprise wild things in the woods, you will need to mind your place and tread gently, with calm alertness and a smooth attitude and presence—don't charge through whatever you encounter.

In time, cultivating this kind of awareness will also make you more aware of the spirits of the trees beyond their physical presence. You'll begin to notice how they feel, what they express, and how they affect the life around them. Some spirits will be open and friendly, while others will be forbidding. Like all living things, spirits are as rich and varied, so try to encounter them on their own terms, as they are. Let certain trees attract you and others ward you away. Spot where some reach to the heights of the sky and others cause shadow all around regardless of their species. Some will welcome you quietly, and others will say "I am here" and push out at the world.

If you are consistent with your practice, over time you will become aware of a tree or a number of trees that attract you and feel good to work with. Note their species, and be aware of the changes they go through: What season are you in? How does it affect them? Then look into whether you can learn their folklore and magical qualities. How does the lore compare with what you encounter?

Holy Wells and Tumuli: Places of Earth Connection

There are always places in any community that naturally have higher earth energy and serpent power than others, and many are associated with water or have a history of spiritual importance to a community. Holy wells are a prime example in Ireland and the British Isles, but they can be found in various forms all over the earth wherever humans settle. Often these sites are associated with local gods, spirits, and fairies as well as the serpent forces in the land, places where the spirits of the otherworld and the deep earth rise to the surface.

Caves and the chambered cairns of our neolithic ancestors as well as the fogous (underground ritual tunnel spaces found in the archaeological remains of Iron Age villages) and other ritual chambers of our ancestors are also places of great power where this serpent force may be tuned in to and gathered. In these places, this energy often comes with little effort—all one needs to do is simply be there. Visiting such places throughout the seasons is another great teacher for revealing to us the changes and spirits that frequent such places.

Spending time in such places and building our relationship with offerings and care (such as cleaning a site of rubbish) is a great way to show the spirits our intentions and the landscape itself that we are its goodly neighbour, worthy of the great power given to us freely.

The Spirit World and the Fairy Faith

While we acknowledge the many varied spirits of nature found across the land and within or composed of the elements, a key relationship in the wild witch's craft is the fairy faith, a term used to describe our relationship with the fairies who are a distinct group of spirit beings found across Ireland and the British Isles as well as across much of northern Europe in various forms. These beings are known by many names, and in some ways it does them and the diverse cultures they come from a disservice to lump them together under the term "fairy," but it remains a useful working title for the number of beings that populate the earth and the spirit realm around us here in Britain and Ireland, beings who are *not* what we would call nature spirits or elementals. These beings are generally social in their habits, living in groups and (often in folklore at least) functioning with their own distinct societies and etiquette, though some are definitely solitary beings.

From Ireland and Scotland in particular are tales of the fairy rades or rides, where they change their dwelling places at the cross-quarter days of Imbolc, Bealtaine, Lughnasadh, and Samhain, when they travel along the fairy roads or serpent lines. In Ireland especially they may travel the fairy roads at any time; such paths are often marked by wells, fairy forts (old archaeological ring forts), or fairy thorn trees (lone hawthorn trees) that it is bad luck and sometimes terribly dangerous for anyone to disrupt, damage, or block. However, magic performed there that has the fairies' blessing may be especially potent.

Fairy roads and coffin or corpse roads are usually the same—sometimes these are called corpse or coffin roads because this was the route people took in times past to carry a coffin to the church or clan burial ground, therefore making these the roads that spirits of the dead walk along. The relationship between fairies and the dead is complicated, but it's common for the dead to be seen with the fairies. The old belief found in the area ranging from Ireland to Cornwall is that the dead go to the realms of fairy and, in time, some even become fairies themselves. These beliefs existed for centuries alongside Christianity and formed an uneasy and often contradictory relationship with Christian belief. Christianity was often the public belief when someone was asked on matters of public reputation, especially when the local powers of the landlords and the clergy were at stake. The fairy faith existed alongside Christianity as a local belief and power structure based on the local gods and spirits who were approached often but not always by way of the cunning woman or fairy doctor. At times of illness bad luck or other trouble, *these* were the people consulted for assistance rather than the church. And if the problem lay with the fairies or other local spirits, the wise woman or cunning man would intervene with the fairies on the human's behalf.

I consider these fairy roads to be arteries of earth energy; energetic rivers of life force that flow across the landscape over and under its surface in undulating arcs, the great dragon or serpent is the sum of these currents of energy, its overarching consciousness so to speak. Ley lines and dragon lines as well as the corpse roads are all variations on these currents, explaining why they were attractive locations for sacred sites and the common locations for naturally occurring sacred sites. They are places where the spirits, fairies, the newly and ancient dead, and other strange phenomena are all found, but they are not good for mortals to stay on for long, hence the taboo against building a house on a fairy road and the folklore of ghosts and poltergeist activity associated with many houses that remain on one.

The Village Church

A witch or wise woman's relationship with the church either as an organisation or a structure in the village varies from person to person, and folk magic is full of Christian imagery and references favoured by some and not so much by others. I use very little Christianity-based folk magic in my practice, but sometimes something gets woven into what I do simply because it works! As a building in the village, the church is often a place of power, especially old ones that were placed in significant positions where the serpent life force of the area was already high. These places also gather power and spirits over the years as places of focused community energy and belief. As such, don't overlook visiting a church, and although I always advocate treating others' beliefs and their temples respectfully, an herb gathered from a churchyard may be especially potent.

Crossroads, Standing Stones, and Other Power Centres

Another locality of power is the crossroads; sometimes these are ancient roads and trackways that may align with the earth's natural serpent currents, but in more modern settings, large open urban crossroads are also sometimes places of power that have simply built up more recently as a result of human activity and their significance to a community, especially apparent where new stone circles and other monuments have been built. These structures may gather power over time that can be tapped, though if you are fortunate enough to live somewhere with ancient archaeological sites or other wilder sites of power, the latter are preferable. A fine example of this are the many standing stones found across Britain, Ireland, and northern Europe that often date as far back as the Neolithic era and seem to have been placed with an awareness of these serpent currents (even if we will never know what this energy was called or how it was perceived at the time), and they have also been able to gather power since their erection due to their cultural importance and from the power of human belief.

⛤ Practicum
Using a Staff to Gather Serpent Currents

This is a simple exercise that can be changed, adapted, and made far more elaborate; however, I believe its power lies in its simplicity and common sense.

When you are ready and have properly prepared and seasoned your staff with oil or another preservative for prolonged use outside (see the section on tools), take your staff out on long walks around your landscape, especially to the places of local serpent power. As you walk, speak to your staff as a friend and ask it to draw up the power from the earth. You can also ask the spirits of the land to help as you visit them. With every step and every time you touch it to earth and lift it up, see your staff gathering up the serpent energy for use later in your magic: There is no upper limit to how powerful this can be.

The Horned One, Bucca, Pwca, and the Folkloric Devil

Some traditional witchcraft and folk magic refer to "old horny" or the devil, a figure comprising a rich and vast tapestry that varies from person to person and tradition to tradition, as Celtic and folk magic were interwoven so densely with superstition and Christianity. Many of the people prosecuted for witchcraft in Scotland during the witch hunts were said to have made pacts or alliances with "the devil," who was often described as a man in black clothing sometimes with goat's horns or stag's antlers. On examination, we see that these versions of the devil have little if anything to do with Christianity and the Christian Satan; instead, they seem to be hazy descriptions of a folk figure perhaps from a forgotten past or even a cult or coven leader. Sometimes this man in black is described as the partner of, or one working in service of the queen of Elphame, suggesting he is more related to the fairy faith than Abrahamic religion. Nonetheless, this figure is often associated with a certain rebellious nature and quite often with maleficium or malicious magic. Initiations with the devil in this context were often described as sexual in nature and relied on making a pact with him for the practitioner to be able to receive their magical gifts and knowledge, as well as sometimes an overt and declared rejection of the practitioner's Christian faith.

There are several things to consider if we want to unpack the figure of the folkloric devil. All our information gleaned from the Scottish witch trials is just that—court documents written as testimonies of people who confessed under torture that they had betrayed their Christianity and became evil. These sorts of testimonies do not allow for much nuance or understanding of different belief systems or what magical practice may have looked like. As evidence, these confessions are biased in favour of the Christian patriarchal court system and the general frenzy and paranoia of the time.

However, the presence of similar figures can be found in folk magic throughout the British Isles. In addition to the devil is the lord of the wild hunt, a fearsome figure who led a race of the dead across the land on stormy nights and is associated with chaos, danger, and the otherworld; the most prominent examples are Herne the hunter in England and Gwyn ap Nudd of Wales and the West Country. Also in Cornwall is the Bucca or sometimes the two sides of Bucca—the Bucca Dhu (the black bucca) and the Bucca Gwidden (white bucca) who rule over winter and summer, life and death. Considered a powerful trickster being, Bucca is sometimes considered in witchcraft practices to be a god who takes on the appearance of a goat, though at other times he is a sea spirit or even a god of fishermen. The horns on the stag are popularly considered to represent his horns. In Somerset, Bucca is lesser known but remembered as Picwinnie (probably drawn from Bucca Gwidden) and is propitiated for luck and safety at sea. Yet another trace remains in the punkies or hinkypunks, our local names for jack-o'-lanterns at Halloween. Just along the coast from Somerset in Wales is the Pwca, another trickster and shape-shifter, who is considered highly dangerous and surely related to the Cornish Bucca. In Ireland is the Púca, surely another cousin or face of this ancient being.

Looking at the variations of a wider tradition here we see a dark, often horned figure who is honoured by native magical practitioners; the figure is considered dangerous, unpredictable, often sexual and fierce in nature, yet beloved and seems to serve as both initiator and guardian to the deeper mysteries. Sometimes and to some people, the figure is partnered with the fairy queen, a partnership key to understanding the energetic power and spirit presence on the land itself. The exploration of "old horny" is a vast subject, too large to take much further here but is worth time and consideration. With a little bravery, we find greater riches than we may have anticipated.

Drawing the Caim and the Four Airts

A key part of folk magical practice is the demarcation of sacred or ritual space. There are plenty of times when this isn't necessary, but there are always times when having a delineated space to work within is sensible for a host of reasons, the least of which is to increase a working's potency. Usually the space is a circle in which helpful spirits are invoked and any rituals take place. Magical circles go back thousands of years and may even be as old as humanity itself as the first natural step to making something a ritualised practice. Just as the seasons turn and the earth spins around the sun, the circle (and the sphere as it is in practice) is a shape that operates within the rhythm and currents of the natural world, as capable of including as it is excluding spirit presences and dimensions of reality.

The circle may be known by different names in folk magic; casting a circle is also known as drawing the *caim* (an Irish and Scottish Gaelic word for an encircling or circular sacred space often enclosed by prayer), laying the witches' compass, and all sorts of variations, each with their subtle nuances. Within the circle, the four directions, four elements, and sometimes the three worlds are also invoked, and the positions and manner in which these four elements are called all vary. I see no right or wrong here though I do want to stress the importance of feeling out for yourself what feels right for you in your own practice with an eye on the whys. Try out different things, and take note of what works best for what you are trying to do and how it relates to your own inner connection to the forces you want to work with.

One way folk magic and some forms of traditional witchcraft varies from Wicca and high magic practices is the lack of need for strongly maintained protection when working. That doesn't mean we see the spirit world as safe—far from it—but we tend to see the world and nature in particular as already sacred, already something spiritual and magical that we are always part of. This way of thinking contrasts with other magical traditions in that we make allies and work with them rather than summoning spirits and demanding they work with us. In that sense, folk magic (or at least how I practice it) isn't something we need to batten down the hatches for. Instead, it demands we go into a deeper level of presence and connection with the world, one that is never separate from the spirits and continually in flux with the other realms as part of its natural state. In this way, our circle, caim, or compass is our ship floating on the waves of multiple worlds at once, in connection with them all.

I like the sense of navigation the term "compass" invokes; to me, the witches' circle is an active space where we navigate the spirit realm, though in fact the word itself in this context more refers to the creating and pacing of the circular space, as in "en-compassing." Today I know a lot of people use this term from the twentieth-century Cochrane tradition of witchcraft but the term is in fact very old and has roots in the Celtic fairy faith, which is where I connect with it.

A good example is from the Scottish "Ballad of Tam Lin," where one version of the tale recorded from oral tradition states that the heroine, Janet, casts a magic circle:

Between twall hours an ane, (between midnight and one)
And filled her hands o holy water, (she filled her hands with holy water)
And kiest her compass roun.[5] *(and cast a circle or compass by pouring the water in a circle around her)*

In this example, we see the "compass" being cast with holy water, one of the many ways it can be performed. The wise woman uses a variety of materials to draw her circle; she may draw it with her finger in the air, pour holy water, scatter herbs or ash, or even draw a line of fire depending on the circumstances and aims of her rite. Most often, merely drawing her foot or her staff around her in a circle is sufficient, as is "treading the mill" or "treading the wheel" or walking around the space in a circular pattern until the space and energy have been created.

---

5. Francis Child, ed., "Tam Lin" *The English and Scottish Popular Ballads, 1882–1898*. (Tam Lin version 39G: Buchans's MSS, I, 8; Motherwells's MS, 595), accessed 2/27/24, https://www.tam-lin.org/versions/39G.html.

Drawing the caim is similar to drawing the compass but involves more movement. The word *caim* (pronounced kime) is Scots Gaelic for a magical circle or sanctuary, itself drawn from the Gaelic words for turning and churning, so we can see that at its root it implies a thing that is moving rather than a static space; we turn and churn the energy within it with movement or chanting. It is usually (but not always) performed with the repetition of prayers or incantations, in addition to more walking circularly around the space usually in a deisil (sunwise) direction. The circle or caim is cast with the energy raised and the vibrations and intentions in the words uttered. We also find the word *caim* in Irish where it is sometimes used to mean an encircling prayer, though these days it tends to refer to turning or churning, like in a melting pot—a good analogy for making magic and raising power!

The combination of movement and sound when drawing a caim is what gives it great power—by this act we are working with a flowing current of energy that is in keeping with the energy flow of life, and can draw on this for our work. The movement may be as simple as pointing the finger and drawing the line in the air while "treading the wheel" (walking in a circular pattern) or performed with a broom or stang and other movements. The chants may be formal and rhythmic or a simple repetition of the intention of the rite—it naturally varies on personal preference and due to the work's purposes or desired outcome.

A suitable chant can be as simple as "may no harm enter here" repeated over and over as the caim is drawn and the circle trodden around and around to build the energy. If you'd like, it may be something more complex. One prayer I like to chant is to call my power in and is something I've adapted and created from several prayers found in the *Carmina Gadelica*:

Power of the eye be mine
Power of the elements be mine
Power of my heart's desire
Power of the surf be mine
Power of the swell be mine
Power of the sap of my reason.
Power of the raven be mine

Power of the eagle be mine
Power of the Fiann[6]
Power of the storm be mine
Power of the moon be mine
Power of the sun
Power of the sea be mine
Power of the land be mine
Power of the heavens![7]

Working in the way described above allows for power and spirit allies to be called upon whilst the energy is being raised for the work, making for very dynamic, energised rituals that allow us to weave our intentions in from the beginning. The whole thing has a single if organic and flowing focus.

Many folk witches use a staff or a "stang." (I do from time to time; the where and why are largely down to my intuition in the moment.) This tool is used as a central point in the compass or the cairn and becomes the crossroads where all things meet, the lone standing stone, the hub of the mill wheel or circle that functions as a centring and directing presence. At other times (and how I work most often), the hub is within the body of the practitioner sitting in the centre of the circle like the world tree or its Irish equivalent, the Bilé, where all things can be contacted. I draw energy up through my body and invoke the three realms of earth, sea, and sky and do any other energy work through myself from this point.

---

6. The Fiann or the Fianna were a mythical band of roaming warriors, usually tasked with righting wrongs and defending those in need as well as keeping the peace. They are featured in a body of Irish legends known as the Fianna Cycle or Fenian Cycle, which focuses on the adventures and heroic deeds of the Fian leader Fionn mac Cumhaill. They have some historical presence as well as their mythical deeds, as they feature in the early medieval Irish law tracts. They were made up of mostly young aristocratic men, and joining a Fiann may have originally been a rite of passage into manhood.

7. My own adaptation and creation, including excerpts from prayers 285 and 288, from Alexander Carmichael, *Carmina Gadelica: Hymns and Incantations* (Floris Books, 1994), 269–70. Originally published 1900 by Oliver & Boyd.

Illustration 2: Spiral Turning Track/the Caim

The Four Airts

Within the caim or compass, folk practitioners often (but not always) invoke the elements and/or the four directions, or the four airts as they are known in Scots Gaelic. The correspondences between each element and direction can vary from person to person and tradition to tradition, but I draw on my Irish roots here and draw mine from the four sacred centres of where the Irish gods the Tuatha Dé came from in the otherworld, before arriving in Ireland: Gorias, Finias, Murias, and Falias. I find these also correspond well with the Scottish four airts, as Scottish and Irish traditions are so closely related, but it's ultimately up to the individual to find what works.

The Scottish term *airt* means "direction" or "compass points": east, south, west, and north. In Irish and Scottish Gaelic folk magic, much is made of going deisil for positive, blessing magic, and tuathal—counterclockwise or against the sun—to banish something.[8] The four directions in Gaelic

---
8. Scots Gaelic for anticlockwise or antisunwise, *Tuathail* in Irish, *widdershins* in English magic.

folk magic align with the four seasons of east, spring; south, summer; west, autumn; and north, winter. I draw further meaning from what this implies—for example, the breath of new life, ideas, inspiration, and thus air are related to spring; fire with the heat of summer and the tempering of the blade of focus and intent; west and autumn with the ocean as the sun sets over it; and north with the cold stone and thus the earth and the ancestors.

As I also work deeply with Neolithic Bronze and Iron Age archaeological sites for my visionary practices, I draw inspiration and guidance in constructing my caim and the guidance I have received from the spirits there. The doorways in many Iron Age and earlier roundhouses were positioned facing east to capture and admit the rising sun, and so it is with my circle. Equally, the north was always the darkest part of the roundhouse and the place where ritual items have been found, including buried remains of ancestors and animals presumably to remain within the house in spirit form. I therefore situate the place of death, winter, and the ancestors in the north, where they prepare for rebirth with the dawn and spring in the east.

Put together, I correspond the directions and their energies thus:

East–air–dawn–spring
South–fire–noon–summer
West–water–sunset–autumn
North–earth–midnight–winter

Practicum
Meeting the Four Airts at the Crossroads

This is a simple spirit journey to help you explore and orient yourself as you work with your caim and the four airts that can also inform you of personal attributions of elements or other correspondences to your four airts. You may find specific guardians, teachers, or animal spirits come to you to support and guide your work. This journey is also useful to repeat on its own from time to time to refresh yourself and to gain new insights about who or what is coming to you along the spirit roads even as you grow in experience.

Sitting in the centre of your cairn or circle, light a single candle before you and place a gift of fresh bread or something else edible before it as an offering.

Take three deep breaths, raising the life force, the earth's serpent energy up through you and into your body, slowly raising your arms as it travels up your spine and into the crown of your head. Keep that connection strong and breathe slowly, guiding your mind back to the practice if it wanders.

In your inner vision, see before you a patch of earth and grass. At your back is a mighty oak tree with roots deep into the earth below you and branches high above you. This is the Bilé—the great tree, the gateway and guardian of the ways. Reach out your hands to touch the rough roots that sink into the earth on either side of you, as if you are enthroned at its feet. Breathe with the oak and let it fade back into your awareness—it is still there as the two of you occupy the same space.

Now you see in your inner vision that you and the tree are in the centre of a crossroads—it may take many forms, but I tend to see it as a place with green hedges and wide fields beyond with lanes emerging from the north, east, south, and west, and sometimes from other directions as well. I also feel a path reaching up above me and down below me with the little crossroads where I sit with the oak being a central sphere or bubble. All is calm here no matter what comes along the roads towards or away from me. Breathe slowly and let your crossroads form around you—feel the sphere as a central point within you and around you, calm and fully present.

Ahead of you is the road to the east—it starts from the edge of the sphere and stretches into the distance. Be aware of how it feels and looks in your inner vision. Now notice what physically lies to the east of you where you sit in the mortal world. See how the two merge and diverge from one another.

Set your inner vision on the road to the east and see a shape upon it coming towards you and say aloud:

I greet you upon the east road!

Let what happens next unfold as it will. Whoever or whatever is in the east to work with you may send a vision or a symbol. It's just as likely that a being may come along the road and speak with you. Be present for what you see, hear, and feel—it will be of great instruction.

In time, the being or spirit upon the east road will return or recede, or you may bid them farewell for now. Once they've departed, turn your attention to the south, to the right of you. In your inner vision, you are still sat in your sphere but now face south. Again let your inner vision reach along the road and see what lies along its farthest horizon. See also in your awareness what lies in the mortal world to the south of you. Once more, see how the two converge and how they differ. Again, you see a figure coming to you from the road to the south and say aloud:

I greet you upon the south road!

Now let the vision from the south unfold as it will, whether in scenes and symbols, words, or an actual being who draws near. Keep your position at the crossroads but learn all you can. When it is time, the being from the south will return or recede or you may bid them farewell.

Turn now to face west. Let your inner vision stretch to the furthest western horizon, and be aware of what lies to the west of you physically—as before, compare and contrast. Take note of what you see. A being takes form upon the west road and comes towards you just as with the others.

Be intuitive and flexible in your interpretations and take heed of how things feel *and* look. Apply all your senses and say:

I greet you on the west road!

Let the encounter unfold as it will in whatever shape it takes. Stay in your position on the crossroads as you let this being and their teaching come to you. And when it is time once more, the being from the west returns or recedes, or you may bid them farewell.

Finally, turn to face north. Let your senses and inner vision expand along the road in this direction. As you do so, remain aware of the land to the north of you in the mortal world, stretching far into the horizon. Be aware of the two, similar and yet different. Again, you see a being coming to you along the road. Paying heed to all your senses, say aloud a final time:

I greet you on the north road!

This being may come to you and converse or show you visions and symbols, just like the others. Whatever happens, let it unfold as it will as a dialogue and deep learning. Be alert and present to all layers of what is communicated to you. When it is time, the being may return along the north road or recede from your inner vision or you may bid them farewell.

Now let your awareness focus a while on your central position at the hub of the crossroad with your back to the Bilé. See and feel the presence of the oak and your position at the sacred centre. Place your hands on the floor and breathe a while, being fully present and as connected or plugged in as possible for a little while.

When it is time to end the journey, focus on the tree—its roots below and branches above—and feel yourself as sheltered but separate from it. Wiggle and tap your toes on the ground where you sit in the physical world. Clench and unclench your hands and feel your heart in your chest. Open your eyes and return fully, eating and drinking to ground yourself. Be sure to record your insights in your journal.

After your working, make offerings of what seems most suitable based on your meetings with the spirits, placing their gifts in their proper places in each direction from where you sat whilst performing it. It's just as fine to place these offerings in the four directions around the outside of your circle if you were outside; if your working was indoors, you could leave them in their places outside of your house.

Over time, make it your goal to learn your landscape and walk in the four directions around your home as far as you can, one direction at a time to learn its ways in search of awareness of all the beings dwelling there along with any special features in the landscape such as hills, rivers, or wells. Let each path be a pilgrimage that honours and strengthens the bonds you have made.

Chapter 3
Magical Tools

The wise woman and cunning man traditionally had an array of tools and magical objects to assist in their work. While the foundation of the practice is in relationships with the spirits and connection with the landscape, there are many ways to anchor that energy into physical items so that it can be used later. We are animists, so we believe that everything around us has a spirit and a host of magical and other virtues that we can work with. In this chapter is a list of some of the things folk magic practitioners may use.

Wands

Wands are used in all sorts of magical traditions, including Celtic and British folk magic to direct the will and energy. The kind of magic they excel at is based on the kind of wood they are made from and the kind of indwelling spirit they carry. Like the staff or stang, a wand can gather up energy but is best used to direct energy raised up and through the body and through the arm, where it joins the wood spirit's virtues and spirits within the wand to direct the magic together.

All woods from all types of tree have their own specific virtues and energies shared with others of their genus, though there is variation depending on where a tree grows and what is around it. (A list of good magical woods appears on page 142.)

Stang or Staff

The stang is a common part of folk magic practice in Britain and is particularly popular in the rural southwest, where I live. A stang or staff is a practical object for walking the wild countryside at night, and it can also serve as a moveable material symbol of the standing stone or world tree, the hub on which the worlds turn. Magical staffs have long been associated with power and can be very effective at gathering and winding up the earth's serpent forces for later use, as well as for directing energy, particularly if the practitioner fashions one using a suitable wood. A variation on the traditional staff, a stang often has a forked end—antlers, ram's horns, or iron horns are common. As symbols of power, the horns signify the masculine principle and can be used to invoke or stand for various forms of the horned god or the very old Celtic symbol of the horned or plumed serpent. Every practitioner has personal preferences and their own interpretation of the imagery and the materials used, but they are always a powerful tool. Sometimes they are shod with an iron cap or a nail that draws up the serpent energy from the land into it or directs its stored energy out the bottom as it strikes the earth.

Some stangs have enough room for a candle to be placed between the horns, which I think represents the life force arisen from the land actively going out into the world via the ligh, though such stangs may not stay alight on a windy heathland, so their practicality is limited.

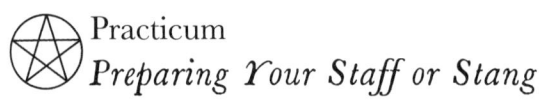

Practicum
Preparing Your Staff or Stang

To prepare, first select a suitable piece of wood that has the magical properties you desire, just as you would with a wand. Knowing the type of tree and ritually gathering or cutting it yourself goes a long way to making your staff your spirit ally rather than a mute object, but this relationship will build up slowly over time and use. When you have cut or otherwise acquired your staff, preserve its wood suitably with oil so that it can be reliably used in the future. Linseed is good for this, although you can steep specially chosen herbs in the oil first to add extra properties to the wood—I like to use mugwort and vervain. You may then like to cap your staff with iron or copper with a specially made iron tip or copper sheath that wraps around the bottom of the staff to protect it and draw in the energy from the earth, or you can coil copper wire around the staff from the bottom to the top. I prefer to leave it bare, but others like iron for this. You can also use a nail—an old iron horseshoe nail is best—and nail it up into the wood and "shoe" it that way so the protective nail draws up power and directs it through the nail into the wood.

Gathering Your Magical Wood from the Wild

In my experience, the best wands and magical sticks are ones that have fallen from the tree and been gathered with its spirit's blessing. The virtues of the tree spirit are then imbued in the fallen wood and become a spirit ally for you to work with. When seeking a wand, it is this quality that makes it powerful; any decoration or personalisation to its appearance only adds to this but will not make much difference if the life and virtue of the tree spirit is not present and willing to work with you. For this reason, it is always best to make and forage your own wands and magical sticks. They can be bought, but they must then be extensively befriended to build the relationship.

To prepare a wand, staff, or any other wood to work with magically, I first suggest spending a great deal of time with the trees. Take many long walks in the woods, and if you are not already good at identifying tree species, take a tree identification book with you to learn. Ideally you can become aware of each tree's "feel": how it grows and where it thrives, the shape and height of the tree, the physical qualities of its wood and bark. These details are the same as learning to recognise a person's face, reading their expressions, personality, and mood.

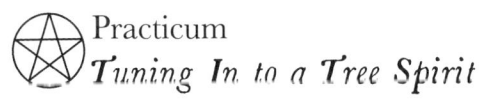

Practicum
Tuning In to a Tree Spirit

When you have found a tree you'd like to work with, spend some time with it. See if you can stand outside the boundary of its branches and feel its totality. Become aware of its whole size and note whether you can be aware of its roots and their reach. Breathe deep and slow and feel in your belly or in your chest what it's like to be in its presence. Does it feel good, bad, welcoming, repelling? Greet it as the venerable being it is in your own way. If it feels right, sit under its branches, ideally with your back to its trunk. Take your time; be slow and mindful. Maintain awareness of yourself as a being with a body and a spirit, and try to align yourself with the tree: Let your back be like its trunk, your head and arms like its branches, your feet like its roots. Sit and be, drinking in the air.

After you've taken some time, be aware that the air you breathe out is what the tree breathes in. Tree breaths are slow, but the pattern of inhalation and exhalation is the same as ours. Be aware of the earth below you both and the sky above. Is it night or day? Feel the vastness of the sky above you and just breathe with the tree.

In time, you may experience deep communion with the tree's spirit, sensing or even seeing it present and communicating with you. Its every gesture and the way it makes you feel to be in communion with it are part of its communication with you. Let it be what it is without placing any need to analyse the experience.

See if you can understand a little of what it needs, how it is in the world. Breathe in as it breathes out, breathe out as it breathes in. Do not worry about the exact exchange of gases; see instead an exchange of energy, of sprowl, or life force. This force can also be understood as the Irish Gaelic *toradh*, the indefinable spiritual essence of yourself, and the tree, merging and exchanging, becoming greater than the sum of your parts.[9] Let your inner senses unfold, and perceive the experience in as broad a way as possible, letting the interchange between you be itself a form of communication. Give things time and let your relationship build. Repeat this exercise and visit the tree often, adapting and adjusting to follow what you experience and what feels right. When the time comes and you want to work magically with its wood, ask it permission. You don't have to make it formal; "Dear tree, may I have a piece of your wood so I can make a staff?" is fine.

After asking, look around for a suitable fallen piece of wood. Be patient, as the right one may take a while to appear. Whatever you do, *don't* cut a piece of wood from it unless you really have to and you are sure you have the tree's blessing. It's best to ask the tree if you may have a certain piece, take

---

9. "Toradh" Teanglann website, accessed 2/27/24, https://www.teanglann.ie/en/fgb/toradh. *Toradh* is found in both Scotland and Ireland where it can mean "fruitfulness," "yield," or "result," but it is also used historically as a metaphysical term to mean the spiritual essence or life force of a thing. It appears in tales of fairies or witches stealing the toradh of crops or milk, meaning that the field would wither, the fruit would have no flavour, or the milk could not churn into butter, their essential quality stolen from them even when their physical matter remained.

time to perceive an answer, and tie a ribbon or string around the particular piece first before you leave and return next time to cut it. That way, the tree can adjust itself so that you do the least or no harm and the sacred, honouring relationship between you is maintained. This is not something that should be rushed! If you ever cut living wood, you must also do so in a tidy and thoughtful way, at a node (a fork in the stick or branch) leaving no ragged edges for disease or damp to get in, and being aware of which direction water will drip, slanting down to the earth rather than into the tree wood so it can heal smoothly.

Practicum
Decorating and Preparing Your Wood

A wand, staff, or other wooden tool can be left as it is with its bark on and no additional decoration—I often leave twigs and everything else attached. However, you can also strip the bark with a knife and sand it down with sandpaper. Know that the wood will dry over time, and you will want to make sure it doesn't dry so quickly that it becomes brittle. Leave it away from direct heat in a place with good circulation. After it has dried, you could then oil it to preserve it and add any decorations or magical sigils. I like to use my own special knife for this kind of work; its use is magical but also highly practical, making it first and foremost a functional knife that is looked after with careful cleaning after every use. I recommend a wooden handled Opinel or something like it bought from a hardware or camping store—I have rarely seen anything so practical in a magical supplies shop! If you have good knowledge of your landscape and what grows around you as well as a good selection of practical tools, you need not buy much to make your own magical equipment and can have the added pleasure of knowing you have made them yourself. They will also be far more powerful.

Scrying Tools

Scrying tools include crystal balls and shewstones, hag stones, black mirrors, as well as fire, flame, and water. Scrying is a powerfully useful tool in magical work, not only for seeing messages from the spirits, possible futures, and glimpses of other times and places but also for developing second sight and general psychic skill. When practiced regularly, the art of scrying is an effective meditative activity that helps still the mind and open up perception. For more on scrying see the divination section, (page 64).

Cauldrons

A cauldron is an excellent tool, useful for all sorts of things. I keep two types: one I can place on a fire that can be used to brew potions and another that serves as a firesafe space to burn a candle or objects within it for spellwork. In addition, I keep several cauldrons—or Dutch ovens—used for anything that will be consumed, such as ritual drink or food.

Cauldrons have always been deeply symbolic objects from the early Celtic period, when they were used as high-status ritual vessels for sharing food, drink, and possibly ritual potions served to a community. They symbolised abundance and the ever-giving womb of the great Mother Goddesses, but they also symbolised the grave; numerous Celtic myths from Ireland and Wales show a cauldron being used to resurrect the dead—thus being a symbol of death and rebirth. Using a cauldron in magic is, in my view, a way of containing what we do outside of time and space. The iron walls of the cauldron contain the magic and therefore this is an excellent resource when burning things for banishing spells or for doing candle spells which neutralise ill will. They also make excellent protective containers for magical tools and ingredients which we want to hold in a neutral or fireproof space.

I have a selection of cauldrons of different sizes from larger, communal and public ritual ones to small ones for candles, but what's most important is what they are made of. A steel cauldron is okay, but iron is better to contain or neutralise baneful magic. Copper or silver cauldrons let the magic pass through their surface, making it best for blessing and charging things. Silver is also protective but in a more active way than iron, adding a positive, blessing, and purifying virtue to the working. Pewter is a cheap option for some work, but don't let it get too hot due to its low melting temperature. If you choose pewter, ensure it is lead-free if you plan on using it for mixtures intended for ingestion.

Practicum
Seasoning Your Iron Cauldron

Every year at Samhain, I bless, reconsecrate, and season my iron cauldrons to protect them from rust and other damage, making sure they are physically clean. I gently sand any rust and cover them with a thin coating of sunflower oil (a thin, neutral oil for this; nothing fancy or with additives). Depending on the cauldron's size and other considerations, I either place it in my oven on a high heat until the oil has smoked off or over an open fire. If you put the cauldron in the oven, be prepared: It *will* get smoky. I shut the kitchen door into the rest of the house and open all the windows as well as use a circulation fan. Once my cauldron is tempered, it will have a beautiful black, shiny finish but must still be left to cool. As it seasons, it gets *very* hot—usually unsafe to touch for at least an hour. Be very careful when you go to check it—don't remove it from its heat source until it is cold. Let the fire die down, let the oven cool. After cooling, I bless my cauldrons with incense; ones used in magical work, I may run under running water—ideally under a living spring—to bless it before carefully drying and storing where it will remain dry as a bone until needed.

Cups, Chalices, Bowls

A ritual cup or chalice is often favoured for sharing drink or for containing an offering of drink for the spirits, usually made of clay or horn, though you can choose any material you like. The ritual bowl is also popular for uses similar to the cauldron, namely sharing food in a rite or placing offerings. Cups and other receptacles are commonly used as more portable versions of the cauldron and often symbolise the womb or represent sacred feminine energy.

It is possible to make or repurpose a ritual bowl or cup—you could carve your own from wood or fashion one out of clay, but even those with less artistic skill can always decorate or personalise something premade. It's just as possible to find what we need in nature; I have a bark "bowl" found in the woods that, while not watertight, is perfect for holding offerings.

Knives

Ritual knives are useful working tools and should be chosen for their practicality first and foremost: for cutting cords, the preparation of herbs, in rituals of severing, or for digging turf or carving sigils. For this reason, a folk witch or cunning woman may have several. An iron knife also features in the fairy faith as a tool for freeing people from fairy, the iron severing their connection with the spirits and setting them free. Just as the cauldron, chalice, or bowl may be understood to represent the sacred feminine, ritual knives and even swords are sometimes used to represent the sacred masculine. Some traditions use the combination of cup and knife to represent sexual union and the calling in of power by placing the knife point down in the chalice. In folk magic, the sexual and gendered elements of these items may be of importance, though it's just as likely for others to have a practice with these items whose focus is purely practical.

Just as with bowls and other items, a ritual knife may be bought as is, be a repurposed knife retuned to magical use, or made by hand on our own, should we have the skill. While iron and other metals have their magical uses, we may make one with wood whittled to our desired shape or find a suitably sharp and elongated stone or even a piece of antler if the knife's use is purely symbolic. For cutting herbs, I'm fond of a bronze knife I found in a specialist garden tool supplier's shop. Everyone is different and has different priorities in their practice. For this reason, magical knives can be found in a vast array of forms, each with their own specific use.

Brooms

Brooms can take all sorts of forms from small handheld bundles of twigs (most often birch) to a full besom broom with a wooden handle. A handheld broom of birch twigs is excellent for clearing a space and spreading around magical smoke from incense as well as for scattering blessed water around a home. They're quite easy to make: Take a thick bunch of twigs and bind with willow whips (thin, whiplike green willow twigs) or twine and trim to make a dense handheld broom you can use to sweep any energy away from a place or person or to "beat the bounds" for protection and defence.

Feather sweepers are a traditional West Country magical tool, usually made with long goose or other bird feathers; I like raven, crow, and jackdaw feathers for this. These tools can be used to sweep away ill will or sweep in good influences, such as sweeping blessings and power towards a person or object. Feathers will impart the specific virtues of the bird upon the sweeper;

crow and raven feathers are particularly powerful, as are swan and hawk feathers, though abide with local laws on collecting feathers found in nature. When ethically sourced and with the bird spirit's blessing, whole birds' wings can also be used as feather sweepers.

A similar tool, the witch's whisk, is also favoured by West Country cunning folk and conjurors. Made by binding blackberry stems together and tying the end together tightly with twine, the stems are dried and the handle is covered with thin layers of wax to make it smooth. The ends of the blackberry stems are burnt as the witch moves around the space to waft the burning blackberry stems to cast out evil influences. A wonderful example can be found at the Museum of Witchcraft and Magic in Boscastle, Cornwall.[10] I have also made whisks with birch twigs, and blackthorn twigs to asperge, dipping into water and flicking them around a space.

The traditional witch's broom is of course a wonderful and famous magical tool. While it is possible to make these from scratch, there are many skilled craftspeople who make them especially, adding fine details and finishing touches. It's both good fun and satisfying to practice making your own broom, but a purchased one can equally be personalised if we add other woods and herbs to the main structure to finesse the details of the particular magic we wish to work. For example, I like to dress my broom with St. John's wort for house blessings at midsummer and add a bundle of blackthorn for banishings that need added power. Brooms may be dressed and decorated with charms and sigils caved, painted, or burnt into the handle.

To use a broom or witch's whisk to banish energies from an area, sweep the energy around the space in a counterclockwise direction to wind down the baneful energy and sweep it out the door, repeating until it is swept fully from the house. You can also sweep a positive or blessing energy into a house by sweeping blessing herbs or incense around a space in a clockwise direction.

The Bullroarer

The bullroarer is an ancient instrument intended for ritual use. A thin sliver of wood is tied with string let out at a length of a few feet and spun over the head resulting in a whirring noise as the wood cuts through the air. It is a

---

10. "Twigs," Museum of Witchcraft and Magic website, accessed February 27, 2024, https://museumofwitchcraftandmagic.co.uk/object/twigs/.

powerful spirit caller, so ancient that wherever it is used, the spirits gather at its call immediately. In Scotland, the bullroarer is known as a thunder spell and was used to protect from lightning.[11] Bullroarers are best if they have been made by the practitioner from suitable wood—oak or rowan, though hazel and ash are also suitable. However, to get the wood thin enough takes skill. If they are not made from scratch, it's important that they are still blessed and decorated by their owner to complete the connection between them and the spirits called.

Pentagrams, Spirals, and Labyrinths

In addition to physical tools, many practitioners also have a slate, stone or other surface upon which a sacred symbol inscribed. This is most often the pentacle, but a spiral, triple spiral, or a labyrinth design are also popular options. These shapes are used in numerous ways. One is as meditation tools where we slow the mind by letting the eyes or fingers trace the pattern over and over, a useful addition when preparing to engage in spirit flight or before spellwork. Equally, we can use the spiral to aid in the charging or empowering of ritual items or as a place where materials for spellwork are laid out.

The pentagram is of course witchcraft's most famous symbol. It symbolises the path of the planet Venus around the sun as well as the five points of the human body, arms and legs extended, and the point facing down can symbolise goat-headed gods such as Pan, Bucca, or Baphomet, or even the animal realm itself. The pentagram is always understood as empowering and protective, casting a protective boundary around whatever is in its centre.

The spiral and triple spiral are found across the world but are particularly prominent in Celtic traditions, where their earliest appearance is on the Neolithic rock art found in Ireland. The shape symbolises many things, but marking the path of energy spiralling inwards to the centre or out into the world are the most relevant here. A spell candle placed in the centre of a spiral can therefore gather energy to it, focus it, and send it out again.

The labyrinth is another a very popular design for focusing and releasing work, especially in the southwest and Cornwall, where examples of it are

---

11. Alfred Cort Haddon, *The Study of Man* (G. P. Putnam's Sons, 1898), 222.

found in rock art near Tintagel. Like the spiral, the labyrinth is a meditative tool that also focuses power inwards to its centre and back out again.

Charging and Consecrating Magical Tools

Once you have an object you would like to work with magically whether it was handmade, bought, or found, you will need to cleanse, charge, and consecrate it unless it is a plant or piece of wood you have already prepared with the spirits. This is an important step that clears it of any previous energy (especially negative energy or spirit presences) and empowers it for magical use.

Items are commonly cleansed using ritual smoke or water or by placing in salt. The method depends on the object and what it is made of. A cleansing incense of juniper, frankincense, or another specifically made incense blend is the best way to cleanse something with smoke, as is wafting the object through the smoke of an outdoor ritual fire. Other items may benefit from water cleaning—a cold tap, or a river or spring is best—with cold and fast-running water. Whereas warmer water holds energy to an object, cold water banishes it; the colder, the better. Some things will feel to you as if they need a good cleanse, such as when a spirit or the emotions of the previous owner is attached to an object (it happens more often than you may think). Covering something in salt works very well, but you will need to decide for yourself how long it should be covered, keeping in mind that the salt may need changing a few times before the object is fully cleansed. At other times, placing something on the earth is a good way to cleanse something instead of salt, as is placing the object on the earth amongst a plant with protective attributes, though this isn't as powerful or ritualised as the other methods.

After cleansing is charging and consecrating the object. The manner in which this is done varies from person to person and depends on the object and what it will be used for. Smaller items may be placed ritually on a pentagram, spiral, or labyrinth, perhaps with other magical items around it or placed under sun or moonlight and left to gather power from the symbol over a span of time. Add more power and intention and charge an item by wafting it through smoke or flame, sprinkling it with charged and blessed water and specially chosen herbs, or sending your own power into it with your intentions using a verbal charm for added power. For example:

I charge and consecrate you, knife, to be a powerful tool,
a blade sharp and true for cutting and preparing my herbs
and for directing my will!

The charm is repeated over and over until it seems the knife has absorbed enough power, after which it is laid on a ritual symbol or a special stone or herbs under the appropriate light to continue charging until you are ready to use it or store it somewhere appropriate. Charged and consecrated items are commonly wrapped in black cloth to contain their energy before and after use.

Although there is no fixed, correct way to do any of this, it is common for rites of consecration to involve all four elements and some verbal instructions to the object to give it magical purpose. But it is far better, in my opinion, to feel an object and do things intuitively rather than read from a book and use our own words. When we're not focused on getting it "right," we can instead immerse ourselves in the work, making what we do far more powerful.

Chapter 4
Divination and the Arte of Finding

Divination is an important part of cottage magic and cunning craft with a great many aspects, from the use of divination cards and pendulums to scrying and divination by other lesser-known means. In this chapter is a selection you may find useful.

Truth Seeking and Spirit Consultation

A key aspect of folk magic or a cunning woman's work is the finding and uncovering of hidden or lost knowledge. In times past, they would commonly seek lost or stolen items or discover who had sent the client ill wishes or maleficium, baneful magic to cause illness or even death. Today we may use scrying, divination, and spirit consultation to perform numerous tasks that may include but are not limited to these methods. Indeed, we may consult with a spirit directly or scry to learn deeper aspects of our craft or seek advice on our spiritual as well as our magical training. In many ways, divination may be considered a way to help us navigate life and its various issues, not only to discern future events; indeed, the future is mutable, dependent on our actions here and now. We can instead use divination with proper awareness and caution to broaden our awareness and help us navigate life in as insightful and informed a way possible.

Scrying

Scrying is often thought of as a key skill in the cunning woman's arte. The most common objects are crystal balls or shewstones, as are fishing weights, dark glass mirrors, and bowls of water.

We may consult the indwelling spirits of the waters to aid us in our scrying or use the water and the effects of light, shade, and reflection to induce a trancelike state to access our own insights. Equally, we may find a special crystal and invoke a spirit into it or ask its already naturally indwelling spirit. We can use the play of reflections upon a black mirror to open a door in our consciousness or merely as a focal point while we calm our minds and allow visions to arise. There are so many ways to do scrying; the best way to begin is an adaptive organic approach that responds to the needs and practicalities in the moment, deepening and increasing skill over time.

Water Scrying

The properties of still water, pools, and lakes are useful in scrying either in situ or drawn and used in a container such as a glass or dark-coloured bowl.

Before scrying, we as practitioners must first undergo ritual cleansing and preparation. We need to be clean energetically and physically to ensure we have created a clear vessel within which we may receive knowledge with as little interference as possible from other energies and intentions. Cleansing can take the form of ritually washing and wearing special robes or a shawl used only for this purpose, followed by an energetic cleanse with herbs or ritual smoke (juniper and mugwort are good for this). Equally, we may feel as though a simple cleaning and tidying of the space used to perform the scrying is all that is required. While this is fine if we are seeking our own inner guidance, more rigorous preparation is advised when conjuring specific spirits for their assistance.

If working out of doors with a body of water, the best place to start is connecting to the land and the powers of place with some meditation and deep, steady breathwork followed by an offering—cream, butter, or a small glass of whiskey are my preferred offerings when in doubt.

Caution: Do not use mugwort if you are pregnant or have menstrual issues.

⛤ Practicum
Scrying with Wild Water

Begin by preparing yourself and perhaps some incense or burning some herbs and an offering at a specially chosen site—for example, a well-positioned rock by the lakeside. Then address the spirit of the water, expressing your respect and a desire to seek vision with them. Here is an example (these words can be modified):

> *Spirit of the waters here, indwelling wisdom of these waters, please attend and consult with me. I offer you my respect and kinship—may I seek knowledge and insight here.*

Sitting where you can clearly see the surface of the water, let your eyes rest and your breath deepen. Present the body of water with your question, speaking aloud. As you do so, gently maintain awareness of any impressions or messages you receive. It may be that you sense or feel the presence of the water spirit and are able to converse; it may be that you find you experience a change of consciousness or awareness and find yourself thinking of your issue in a new way. Be aware of any impressions you get—images, sudden thoughts, or symbols that spring to mind or that you discern in the surface of the water and the play of light as the sky reflects upon it.

⛤ Practicum
Water Scrying at Home

If you wish to do your scrying at home or away from a water source, leave your offering and address the spirit of the water in the same way: Ask for permission to gather some for your scrying and that its indwelling spirit assists you. Once you sense it gives permission, gather the water and store it in an appropriate container until you are ready to use it.

Prepare yourself for scrying as described in the preceding practicum with ritual cleansing and energetically cleansing your space either in a formal magical circle or with cleansing it and seeing it blessed in another way.

Now prepare your water and the container you will use for your scrying. There are several containers I like to use for this, though I choose in the moment, often intuitively and themed depending on the situation. Don't feel limited by a lack of exclusively magical equipment; choose something respectful to the spirit and the task at hand—if you do not own something specifically for this purpose, the best bowl in your kitchen works perfectly.

One thing I like to do is add a symbol or sigil; usually for scrying I add the symbol of the moon and ask that the moon bless my scrying and ask the indwelling spirit of the water to attend me. At times, I have received intuition on specific sigils to use regarding specific bodies of water directly from the spirit themselves—these have no previous traditional basis and have just come to me, and you may find the same happens to you from time to time. You can also use angelic or other sigils if that's how you like to work. I tend to only use Abrahamic forms of magic very sparingly as my work is centred more on my Celtic and Pagan/pre-Christian leanings, but the cunning folk of the past often mixed magical techniques from several traditions as well as their own senses and inner vision.

After drawing the symbol of the moon on the container, I then pour the water into it, asking as I do so that the moon and the water spirit assist me. At other times, I may draw the symbol on the water's surface with my fingertip, repeating the motion over and over with some chanted prayers whilst resting my eyes upon the surface until I feel the energy build sufficiently and the water spirit make itself known.

I tend to create my prayers on the spot, though what follows are some good ones from tradition I also use. You might like to try this one repeated over and over until you sense the water is ready:

Spirit of the living waters come to me here,
guide and advise me in truthful kinship.

When it feels right, you will naturally feel the shift in consciousness and the power build—you may sense the presence of the water spirit or catch a glimpse of an image or flickering light within the water. Let your mind be calm and clear, and ask your question or questions, seeking dialogue with the water spirit, if possible. Be open to all forms of communication. You may feel impressions rather than receive words or images; everyone is different, and no way is better than another. After all, it is the mind that translates these messages from the spirits, and just as we are all unique, our translation devices are all a little different too!

⛤ Practicum
Moon Scrying

The moon can be used to enhance many kinds of divination and oracular practices, especially scrying, which is a way of seeking visions using a physical object, like a crystal ball, or, here, a bowl of water. If you've not tried it before I advise you to also take time meditating on the moon to develop your visionary skills.

You will need a dark coloured (preferably black) bowl and some spring water. You may also like to add a few drops of oil. Mugwort oil is best but an essential oil such as frankincense in a carrier oil (almond, grapeseed, et cetera) also works. Place a few drops on the water's surface so that it swirls and gives the water a sheen. You will also need a darkened room or a single candle.

This scrying is best performed when you can see the reflection of the moon in the water, so position yourself accordingly. However, if you can't perform this on the full moon, you could also perform by the light of a single candle.

Prepare your space so that it is dark and calm, and make sure you will be uninterrupted for at least thirty to sixty minutes. Position yourself so that you are sitting comfortably with the moon's (or candle's) reflection on the water's surface.

You may decide on a specific question or just use this technique to see what you can see. Scrying takes practice and patience, but with time, all sorts of things will come to you, usually in symbolic imagery or in a sense of suddenly receiving messages.

Slow your breathing and rest your eyes on the water. If you have a question, ask it aloud to the light source, repeating the question nine times (nine is a sacred lunar number) with your eyes firmly but gently unfocused on the reflection. Your surroundings should be dark enough and you sitting near enough so that your own reflection is dark and vague in the water and the light of the reflected moon or candle blurs slightly as you rest your focus. Let your mind grow calm and receptive. Let your thoughts drift gently, occasionally pulling them back to your question but mostly allowing your consciousness to shift slowly with calm breath and softly focused eyes. Feel your heartbeat slow to a gentle, calm beat.

If you work with any spirit guides or allies, let some time pass and then ask them about your question, keeping your eyes softly focused on the moon's reflection. You may find certain feelings flow over you as your state of consciousness changes in a state of gentle trance or as an answer in and of itself. It's equally possible to experience physical sensations or see images flash into your mind. Be open to receiving whatever messages come in whatever way they come. You may have to use some abstract thinking to draw all of the meaning from your spirit messages, but they will come to you.

After spending time where you are, thank the moon or the candle as well as your guides and allies. Be sure to ground yourself well afterwards, and record your experiences in your journal.

Shewstones

Traditional shewstones or "show-stones" are most often crystals or crystal balls, though the name sometimes also refers to other stones such as hag stones, marble spheres, natural white quartz pebbles, and glass fishing weights used for scrying. There are two possible things happening when a cunning man or wise woman uses as shewstone. The first is the practitioner is being aided in far seeing (also called remote viewing), gleaning knowledge of a person or event from afar. Remote viewing can be distant in time, future or past, or in space at a great geographical distance. This operation is usually assisted by the stone's indwelling spirit. The second thing that can occur is that the indwelling spirit is consulted directly and the stone itself is the locality for the magical activity; consultations with the spirit and even magical working may take place within the stone itself as a kind of access point to the spirit realm or otherworld.

Not every crystal or crystal ball works as an effective shewstone. What works and what doesn't seem to have little to do with the kind of crystal or stone used, though purity and clarity seem to have an effect. Clear or white quartz or, conversely, black crystal-like obsidian seem to be the most effective. Neither crystal colour implies any kind of morality or the practitioner's type of magic; ultimately, both are good places upon which to rest the eyes and let the other senses come into play. The most important detail is hardest to define—sensing a helpful spirit who wishes to work with you through it. Assessment comes down to individual aptitude, skill, or experience.

Practicum
Scrying with a Shewstone

To prepare a shewstone, first wash it tenderly, presuming it is not a water-soluble crystal. Anoint it with a little precious oil as an offering and to sanctify it—I like to use high quality frankincense essential oil or mugwort oil that I have prepared myself.

Caution: Do not use mugwort if you are pregnant or have menstrual issues.

Next, speak to the spirit in the stone. I ask the indwelling spirit to come forth to show me truthfully the answers I seek and am then specific about which questions I ask and how, something I have thought about beforehand. For example:

Far-seeing spirit of this stone, good helper, show me truthfully the answers I seek without any illusion. I ask of you to show me what ails my client (insert name) of (insert address) who is the son/daughter of (insert parents' names). Answer me truthfully: What ails them and what do they need?

Then allow yourself to settle into communion with the spirit in the stone and let your eyes rest on its surface. When I do this, I may have flashes of vision or enter a dialogue in which the answers are revealed.

This procedure can also be used to seek advice and assistance from other dead cunning folk and advisers generally on how to improve your skills in the craft.

Fishing Weights, Witch Balls, and Dark Mirrors

Both coloured glass fishing weights (also known as witch balls) and dark mirrors are usable for scrying, and both are worked with in similar ways. If they can be opened, fishing weights and glass baubles can be used to entrap spirits and filled with suitable material as discussed elsewhere (see the chapter on protection), making them also suitable as spirit homes for welcome spirits to dwell within for our assistance just as with shewstones. These spirits may be carefully chosen—for example, invoked beings of the Enochian magic tradition—just as easily as they can be whichever spirits dwell in our localities whom we ask for assistance. Personally, I find building relationships with nature and ancestral spirits and asking them to assist me via the fishing weight or shewstone to be the most useful and powerful, as there is a more organic process built on mutual good will and trust. As an example, I may seek the assistance of a spirit purely for my scrying work found in spirit flight and called on during the use of various scrying and divination techniques who may dwell in the fishing weight as long as they wish and when called. The same goes for dark mirrors, which are often made from obsidian or glass painted black. The use of these tools is similar to working with shewstones in that they require an initial ritual cleansing and sanctifying after which time is taken to enter a trancelike state to commune with the spirit within.

Practicum
Spirit Flight to Seek a Scrying Spirit Ally

This practice may take many attempts to be fully successful and will need ideally to be adapted and intuited to the individual doing this work, though the template of the working is straightforward.

At the dark moon, seek a quiet place to perform the work and create a caim or sacred safe space. Prepare yourself with ritual cleansing and prepare an offering—a libation of whiskey or milk or a small cake are my preferred offerings, unless I know what a specific spirit would like.

Light a single candle and sit upright. Breathe slowly as you steadily let yourself settle into a light trance, resting your eyes upon the flame. In your inner vision, see yourself walking upon a rough earthen path between hedges, the sky above you bright with stars. You gradually see a shape ahead of you that, as you approach, you can see is a tall standing stone marking the central point in a crossroads, one path of which you have been walking. Take a moment to examine the stone and feel your presence at the crossroads before calling out that you seek an ally and friendly spirit with whom you may scry to serve as a trusted and honoured adviser.

In time, a form will come to you along one of the paths and meet you at the standing stone. Ask them first: Will they assist you with your scrying with true answers? Pay careful heed to their response, trusting the first impression you get. Next ask them if there is good will between you, and again pay close attention to their response. Finally, ask the being how they will work with you, listening carefully to the fine details of their response and your gut feeling about the encounter. Remember that if you feel uncomfortable at any point, you need not work with or call that spirit again and can seek another.

After enough time has passed such that you feel you know what you need to to work with this spirit again, bid it farewell and return the way you came.

Remember to ground yourself well afterwards with eating and drinking, and to record your experiences in your journal for later use.

Fire Scrying

In addition to scrying with water or objects, you can also scry with fire. People have used fire as a way to read messages from the spirit world since the earliest times. There's something about a fire in a hearth or outside when the night becomes late and those present naturally grow quiet and introspective as the flames turn to embers, when it is easy to sink into a receptive mood and read what the fire, this venerable being, wishes to communicate.

Practicum
Fire Scrying

If you have access to an indoor fireplace or can light a suitable fire outside, light it with care and respect, thanking it and asking the spirits of the flames to show you what you need to see at this time.[12]

For lighting ritual fires, I like to gather all the materials I need beforehand—fire lighting material, tinder, kindling, and fuel. I like to light a fire using flint and steel or a fire striker, but getting these to work can be tricky if you haven't practiced; matches or a lighter are perfectly acceptable to use. Whatever your method, lay your fire with care and thought and perhaps make some offerings of flowers or a sprinkling of incense. Pause for a moment and consider the purpose of your fire. Light it with your intent in mind along with a prayer for its effectiveness and to show respect to the fire spirits. For example:

> *I light this fire now and give you life, fire spirits,*
> *That you may show me wisdom from the realms beyond,*

---
12. Extensive details about lighting a ritual fire appear in *Wild Magic* (Llewellyn Publications, 2020).

That I may see in flame and ember what I need to see at this time, truth revealed, the breath of other otherworld in your smoke, the light of the land within your flame. May this scrying fire bless my vision and make it true.

Light the fire and tend to it carefully until it is going, and then let it burn for a while. You may like to use this time to sing songs to the fire or to chant—let yourself sink into a space where you relate to and feel in connection with the fire, always taking safety into consideration.

Let the fire burn down in its own time as you gently speak with it. Share with it how you are doing, what is going on in your life, and whatever you may need help with. You could choose instead to ask it formal questions, but I advise working on your relationship first and foremost. Assistance offered is more powerful than help demanded. Let your own spirit settle and your eyes rest upon the flames and embers. Your thoughts and imagination roam gently, floating on the movement of light and shadow. Don't push for answers—instead, feel the body language of the fire, its mood and tone, to let your intuition and inner vision follow it gently, allowing insight to arise in your mind as well as watching to see if you see any patterns images and symbols appear in the flames.

Smoke Scrying

Smoke from fires or incense can be used for scrying in the same way as fires, and the process is much the same: Let your mind relax and stay gently aware of any shapes, symbols, or body language you may sense in the smoke's movements.

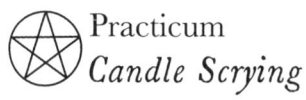

Practicum
Candle Scrying

This practice is a simple form of fire scrying; the art is in how it is read and interpreting what is seen. Sitting alone in a darkened room free of drafts, take a fresh candle. Using a fresh match, strike it and light the candle. As you do so, be aware that a new fire spirit has been created: Greet it as an ally. Ask it to assist and grant you insight at this time.

Sit back at a good enough position so that you are near the candle but not so close that your breath affects the flame. Ask it to advise you about a particular issue; a clear, singular issue yields the best results. Talk about your concern and then go through the possible answers, presenting the flame with one scenario after another. Let yourself sink into a meditative state and feel as you gently enter into a dialogue with the flame, paying particular attention to any movement of the flame and any light effects—these can be read like body language and gesture. Equally, you may find ideas, symbols, words, or visions come to you. Be open to any form of communication, including flashes of insight that may come later.

Coscinomancy: Sieve and Shears

This is an ancient form of divination that essentially works rather like dowsing and is used to find things that have been lost or stolen—if stolen, it can also identify a thief.

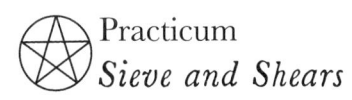

Practicum
Sieve and Shears

This divination is tricky to perform, but even the difficulties you may have can be interpreted as an answer to your question. The sieve this technique requires is an old fashioned agricultural or gardening sieve shaped like a metal drum as well as an old-fashioned set of agricultural shears. The shears are opened up wide enough that they can grip the rounded metal sides of the sieve (so that looking from the front it looks like a circle with the X or V shape of the shears on top) and these are lifted together using only one finger on either side of the shears just beneath their handles. A prayer is then recited—traditionally to the Catholic Saint Paul, but Saint Anthony was also a favourite as the patron saint of lost objects. Today we may pray to the goddess Brigit or simply ask our helping spirits.

The sieve will slowly rotate either clockwise (a yes) or anticlockwise (a no), or it will move side to side for a maybe or ask again. The manner in which we read the results is dependent on intuition, repeated practice, and a good relationship with the assisting spirits.

You can use a small modern kitchen sieve and scissors instead of the agricultural sieve and shears; some practitioners instead suspend the sieve from a piece of thread to use it as a pendulum.

Illustration 3: Sieve and Shears

Bibliomancy: *The Bible and the Key*

Another popular folk divination practice is the bible and key, but really any book can be used so long as it holds emotional significance to us so that we can draw on the power we have given it. Of course in times past, people believed it was the unique spiritual qualities of the Bible that made this effective, so it's a matter of personal preference if you like to use Christian elements in your work or not.

This form of divination also works a lot like a pendulum, although the movement is less obvious and it takes a bit of working out to decide what movement means what.

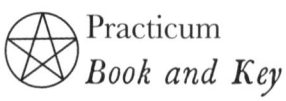

Practicum
Book and Key

For this practice, you will need a book, a large key, and a length of strong twine. Open the book at random. If you are using a religious book, you can select a particular passage; in the Bible, Psalm 49 is one common choice, though

I don't use the Bible for this. Instead, I like to use a huge herbal directory as a gathering of plant spirits and place the key in the book with its handle end sticking out. Bind the book tightly with the twine so the key can't fall out. Then lift the book between your thumb and forefinger from the handle of the key, and ask your questions. The book will sway like a pendulum weight.

I always ask my spirit allies to assist me with this work, but as already stated, some may find the Bible has an inherent power to assist them. After all, folk magic is practiced by all sorts of people, including those with Christian leanings—it's a dogma-free practice, open to everyone.

Tasseomancy: Reading Tea Leaves

Tasseomancy or the reading of tea leaves is a wonderful and social way to scry, making it a type of divination perfectly suited to the kitchen table when people come to you with their troubles.

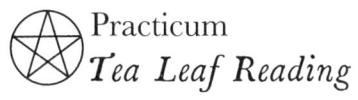

Practicum
Tea Leaf Reading

There are numerous guides to tea leaf reading, but the general idea is that you make a pot of tea with tea leaves, and as it is poured, let the leaves fall to the bottom of the cup. While it is drunk, the reader and client discuss what is happening and what may be needed. When the only things left are the leaves and dregs, let your mind settle and look into the cup for any symbols. Alternatively, you can divide the surface of the cup in your mind's eye into a circle of twelve parts, each part signifying an astrological sign. Then examine what tea leaves lie where according to this and take note of how the parts relate to each other.

Oneiromancy: Dream Interpretation

Wise women and folk healers have always paid heed to their dreams and the dreams of those who come to them for help. Dream interpretation is tricky because of course we all have many layers of dreams, from sorting the daily events of our lives to the deeply significant ones that reflect our inner life and messages from the spirit world. In some ways, the key to discerning what is and isn't a spirit dream doesn't lie so much in a dream's details so much as in the dream's feeling; that is, how it feels to us when we wake and what stays with us about it during the day. That said, there are a great many guides to dream interpretation, and certain symbols and images have long-held associations and meanings that we can apply to this subject if we find them helpful.

Here are a few key traditional dream symbols:

Absent loved ones: If ill, they are in difficulty; if well, they thrive.

Angels: Peace and goodness.

Bees: A swarm suggests you are well respected. To dream of being stung means trouble with a friend or abandonment by a loved one.

Bells: Bells ringing signifies good fortune prosperity and marriage.

Cats: Traditionally dreams of cats warned of an untrustworthy woman around you.

Dancing: Fortune and good luck.

The dead: Dreaming of the dead may mean they are contacting you, or news is coming.

Eggs: When broken, signifies a poor change of fortune.

Fire: Frustrations being released; new things coming.

Fish: Luck in love.

Flowers: Good things; prosperity.

Garden: Success in love.

Glass: Broken glass means family strife.

Hares: Misfortune; deception.

Horses: Prosperity and health.

Jackdaw: Danger; malicious people.

Kiss: Be careful whom you trust.

Knives: An ill omen.

Lightning: Luck, power, prosperity, and success.

Magpies: Marriage.

Nightingale: Ease from anxiety.

Nuts: Money.

Rain: Misfortune.

Sea: When clear and calm, favourable; murky or stormy suggests misfortune or dispute.

Silver coin: Be careful of your money; lunar associations.

Wedding: A funeral.

Yew tree: Death of an elder.

Dowsing

Dowsing is an excellent practice used for centuries to divine all sorts of things from finding lost objects to tracking earth energies. Dowsing to discern who was sending malicious magic or to find things that had been stolen and by whom was a large part of the cunning folk's job in times past, but this highly adaptable method can still be used today for a host of things relevant to our practice, and every magical practitioner should know how to do it.

There are two main methods to dowse: with a pendulum or dowsing rods. A pendulum is good for indoor question-and-answer sessions, whereas dowsing rods are more useful for working out on the land and divining earth energies and water sources.

Pendulums

Pendulum dowsing is very straightforward. You can easily find pendulums for sale, but anything suitably weighted on a strong thread or fine string will work, such as a ring. I like to use a small hag stone suspended from about eighteen inches. There are two schools of thought regarding how this works: either the spirits move the pendulum—one in the pendulum itself or one who has independently arrived—or we make the pendulum move subconsciously with subtle movements of the body that express a truth we aren't able to consciously articulate yet. I think it's a bit of both! First, talk to the pendulum and agree how it will show you the answers you seek; the most common are a simple clockwise circle for a yes, anticlockwise for a no, side to side for both, and back and forth for neither. Hold the pendulum up by its thread and ask it to show you its yes, no, and so on so that its movements confirm how the answers present themselves in the future.

Next, ask the pendulum a series of clear yes/no questions to narrow it down to the answer you seek. For example, "Has my watch been stolen?"

may yield a no. Moving on, next you would ask, "Have I lost it?" If you receive a yes, ask additional questions: "Did I lose it in the house?" "No." "Did I lose it in the car?" "No." "Did I lose it at the gym?" "Yes." "Has it been handed in?" "No." And so on.

Dowsing can also be used to divine the presence and intentions of spirits around us in magical workings as well as the best ways to deal with them. Dowsings are also helpful in healing sick buildings and helping us detect energy flows if we use them instead of rods. Good dowsing gets better with practice, so persevere until it becomes easy to do.

Dowsing with Rods

There are two types of dowsing rods. The oldest and most traditional is a forked hazel stick of about three feet in length, with the forked end wide enough to hold steadily with hands a good distance from the join. This type of rod is best gathered ritually with care for the hazel spirit, freshly cut. It is used by holding it out with the length in front of the body parallel to the ground with elbows close but not tightly held at the sides. The forked end is held firmly but not tightly.

This method, walking with the forked rod directly before you, is best used to track water or energy courses across an area of land. A good way to do it is to chart a course in your mind's eye back and forth across a space in a loose grid pattern, head up and walking at a slow but steady pace with the rod out in front of you. It will dip suddenly to the earth when it comes across water or some other current under the earth's surface. Usually it detects earth energy, but it has also been known to detect minerals and geological patterns. I have seen dowsing be effective in this way for all sorts of people, including those who had no belief in its efficacy whatsoever. It just works, and there is no particular ritual involved.

I was fortunate to be taught dowsing in this traditional manner to chart water courses and divine where to dig a well by a very old man on the Isle of Islay in the Outer Hebrides in my late teens. It was an extraordinary experience to chart where the water flowed across the land and see where it reached the beach to flow into the sea. This elderly gentleman was employed to divine where to dig a well for a house and was well respected and successful. He told me at length that dowsing was a skill used in that area for centuries, long before anyone there could get hold of technology to locate these things.

With a little practice you can ask the hazel questions to fine-tune your discoveries, but its best use is this ability to map the energies and water flow in an area. Such mapping can help you discover fairy and other spirit roads and ensure you work in alignment with rather than against these natural currents.

Metal Dowsing Rods

The other form of dowsing rods are L-shaped pieces of thin metal, the short part of the L being large enough to comfortably but loosely be gripped in the hands with the longer part of the shape about a foot or so long, held parallel to the earth above the handle end. Using these dowsing rods is similar to using a hazel rod, only they will swing from one side to another or cross at various energetic points on the earth instead of dipping suddenly. The swinging and crossing motions can be quite useful and may assist in helping you chart an energy flow by steering you around an area and then showing you where energy converges, goes deeper, or rises when the rods cross. By asking questions of the rods, you can fine-tune how you read what they are telling you, so to speak. This will be different person to person, with slightly different styles of expression and interpretation arising over time, so be patient and have fun practising.

Metal dowsing rods are often made from copper or bronze, but I've seen them made from wire coat hangers that work just as effectively in an experienced dowser's hands. There is definitely a little bit of art to good, useful dowsing, but just as with hazel rods, I've seen this be effective even when used by sceptics!

Chapter 5
Apotropaic Magic:
Household Protections and Wards

The relationship with our homes is central in a magical life. If we feel we have a place to be that is just our own private space, it can be liberating… or something that restricts and constrains us, depending on where we are in our journey and how suited we are to that environment. We all need to have somewhere totally safe and inviolate, and if we are lucky, our homes can be just that. If they aren't, we must work to maximise and improve our spaces' positive qualities.

Every home has its own nature and spirit as well as its own flow of energy around the space. Sometimes our homes don't have a flow that works well and encourages stagnation or moves the energy too quickly out of the home. Equally, some houses have stuck spirits or echoes of previous occupants still lingering; sadness, grief, trauma can all linger in a home if left unaddressed.

Warding and Banishing

There are many reasons for us to keep our homes spiritually and magically protected, and wards and protections were once one of the cunning man or wise woman's main tasks and is still something that many clients frequently ask me about. Sometimes a house is situated in areas that gather negative energy due to their position in the landscape or their history—sometimes full-space clearing rituals can be good, or deep work healing the area's land spirits is the answer. At other times, we simply need to step up in needed magical housework to keep the energies clear, especially in built-up areas or if we are facing difficult circumstances or situations. Stress, fear, illness—all sorts of things can require paying attention to our psychic hygiene to keep ourselves and our spaces in optimal health. It's also possible to attract maleficium, the conscious ill will of others, which can have a powerful detrimental effect on our well-being as well as the home's energy. Such ill will isn't usually deliberate, but anyone holding those bad feelings is aware of how they feel, and it is still powerful—jealousy and resentment can be dangerous if left unchecked and undefended against. In fact, those negative emotions were and are a major source of psychic or magical attack. Although much more rare, there is also the possibility of deliberate maleficium—magical attack from other practitioners. All said, this is less likely than people often fear, and the sort of people who engage in that kind of practice usually sow the seeds of their own downfall. Nonetheless, there are many ways for us to step up and keep ourselves and our homes safe from these energetic intrusions and keep a calm, beneficent atmosphere around ourselves and our environments.

Boundaries

One of the first considerations of boundaries is a matter of common sense: Who do you let in to your home? What kind of environment do your actions encourage? Using discernment is one of the most important first steps for keeping yourself and your life energetically clear. If you don't trust someone and know they also do magic, don't let them in your home or share private knowledge of yourself with them, similar to anyone who makes you feel unsafe or disrespected. Remember that it's important to take ownership of your space. Sometimes if a home is haunted or filled with negative energies, its occupants may find themselves shrinking in the area, feeling as if they can't fully occupy the space psychologically and psychically. A classic example is feeling afraid at night in bed and wanting to hide under the covers. If you ever feel like this—even if you're not haunted but feel afraid due to the eerie play of light on the wall or a robe hanging on the back of the door—don't let yourself shrink and hide. Take ownership of your situation: Get up, turn on the light, and go move the robe or whatever's feeding your uneasiness. The same goes if you feel the cause of your feeling of fear is supernatural or magical in origin: Take charge of your situation and proceed with steps to protect yourself and your space.

Iron

One of the most famous items in British folk magic is the horseshoe. Made of iron, it is naturally protective and can have a powerful banishing energy if necessary. As a protective talisman, a horseshoe is nailed over the entrance to the house; some traditions say with the ends turned upwards to hold luck, while others say prongs downwards to earth ill intent. I tend to favour prongs up when nailed to an entrance though it depends on what I'm using it for. The horseshoe can also be placed in water at the full moon, and the water used to mark and defend boundaries over the coming month.

Iron nails are also very useful in folk magic. They can be added to witch bottles and charm bags to ward away ill wishing and unwelcome spirits or used as acupuncture needles on wax figures for healing and releasing sickness or even for cursing, directing ill will to the body parts they puncture.

Written protection or healing charms are also sometimes wrapped around large iron nails and buried or placed under floorboards. The iron in these spells serves to banish sickness or ill will focused in the way the written charm describes. Iron nails can also be placed in the earth around the four directions of the home as wards against malicious magic or unwelcome spirits. This practice has been found to be very successful when living near a churchyard or a known haunted location such as a disused prison or a gallows tree. The iron forms an energetic web around the space where no negative energy may enter. This sort of work must be balanced by deliberately drawing in blessings to balance it or you will end up with a stagnant atmosphere and few visitors.

Practicum
Iron Water

Iron water can be used to mark boundaries or to ritually cleanse items or spaces. It can also be added to bathwater to remove bad energies or unwelcome spirits from the body and personal space.

Take an iron nail or horseshoe and submerge it in fresh spring water. Leave it to steep for several days or up to a month absorbing sunlight. Thank the iron and water spirits as you do, telling them that you want to make a protective potion that will banish all negative presences and energies.

When you believe the water is ready, take the iron object out of the water, and pour the water into a sterile, dark bottle. Store it in a cool dark place for whenever it is needed but do not ingest it. Replace it with a fresh batch every few months.

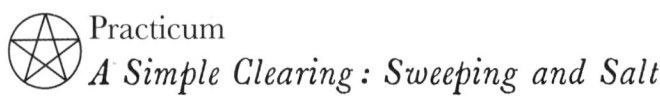

Practicum
A Simple Clearing: Sweeping and Salt

One of the first and easiest things you can do is guard and cleanse your boundaries with sweeping and salt. With a broom (a witch's broom or a household broom), sweep the whole space. Starting with the place furthest from your doors and working towards them, dust and clean so that you sweep all the dust and accompanying bad energy or even spirits out the door together. Get creative and energetic with this, sweeping cobwebs from the ceilings and swooshing your broom through the air, demanding out loud that all uninvited or unwelcome spirits leave.

Speak clearly and with intent—you don't have to use fancy language. Try this:

This is my house and domain; I demand that all uninvited and unwelcome spirits and energies leave here immediately!

Keep saying or even shouting your words whenever it feels right, sweeping as you go. Listen to your intuition and instincts to pay special attention to anywhere you think unwelcome spirits may be lingering. Be aware that they may well move around the space to avoid banishment, so be systematic about your space and see that you harry and guide the energy out towards the door and across the boundary. When you get to your front or back door, open it and sweep the energy and any unwelcome spirits through it—stand to the side to let them pass and say out loud:

All unwelcome spirits must leave here now!

Really mean it—this is your space and you control it. Next, get some salt and mark your boundaries. Draw a line of salt across all outside doors and along the outside of all the window ledges. Exterior gates, garage doors, and any other boundaries should also be salted. You can use table salt if you have nothing else to hand, but it can be strengthened by adding other protective herbs and empowering them before use. In some cases where you are new to a place or do not have everything close by, I advise using table salt and then gathering what you need and doing an even more thorough job the next day or when you have everything.

Crossing and Hex Breaking

Sometimes when things feel off in our environment, we have a run of bad luck or are beset with bad dreams or low energy or, even worse, keep getting the feeling something unwelcome is in the house. If this is the case, it may be time to consider whether someone has sent bad energies or a deliberate hex in our direction. Hexes are a delicate matter, requiring us to take steps to make sure we don't let paranoia or unfounded suspicion about someone make things worse or create a conflict where there was really none before. If we stay calm and in alignment with our ethics, we can still take steps to break any hexes or curses sent against us without sinking to the same level.

Practicum
A Candle Hex Breaker

Gather a black candle and a holder in which you can safely burn it all the way down. Gather a magical or craft knife and some salt.

Create your sacred space. It's best to cast a circle and call in all the protective spirits you work with—spirit allies, plant kin, animal allies, and so on.

Sitting calmly, use the divination technique of your choice to get a feel of what the situation is and who may be sending ill will your way; dowsing (see page 77) is ideal for this, or you could try vision work. If you get a clear sense of where the trouble is coming from, take the knife and inscribe the person or group's name upon it. If you are not sure who or where it is coming from, inscribe the words "my enemy" upon it.

Place the candle in a place where it can safely burn all the way down, and surround it in a circle of salt. Taking a fresh match, light the candle and stare into the flams, using your breath to raise up your power from the earth. When you are ready, speak to the flame:

> *I speak to you flame spirit and black candle: May you hold all the ill will sent to me and burn it, burn it down to nothing. Gather up all the curses and darkness sent to me and transform it to light; take their hate and burn it, burn it down to nothing. Here I name the ill will of [name or "my enemy"] towards me and command it now to be burnt till nothing more of it exists and it does me no harm. Their power is nothing and their intention is nothing. Their power against me is burnt down to nothing, burnt to nothing burnt to nothing, and the harm they cast out is burnt to nothing burnt to nothing burnt to nothing.*

Repeat until you feel your will has settled into the candle and the flame.

Take great care while the candle burns down to nothing. When it is completely burnt, take any trace of wax and throw it away in a public bin together with the salt. After disposing, wash your hands in fresh salt water. If no wax remains, throw away the salt: Flush it down the toilet or, if it is only a small amount, throw it into a fast-running river.

Practicum
Cord-Cutting Spell to Sever Energetic Bindings

Sometimes we may feel bound or someone may come to us who seems to be somehow attached to their enemy or has become emotionally stuck in their attachment to someone or something, an ex-partner, failed business, or perhaps even a spirit of a dead person where the connection is preventing both parties from moving forwards. It's also possible for magical practitioners performing maleficium to bind someone to limit their power or ability or even draw them in as a lover. While rare, it can happen. In such instances, a cord-cutting ritual is helpful to sever those unhealthy energetic connections.

This practice is best done in a safe ritual space such as a cast circle or caim with plenty of protections around you. You will need to burn protective and banishing incense to keep up your energetic hygiene, in addition to a ritual knife, salt, a black candle, and about a foot's worth of black thread. If you can do this next to a lit fire, all the better.

When you have created your safe, sacred space, call in any spirit allies and protective powers you would usually work with. Raise your energy up from the earth and cast a circle of salt around your candle and light it. As you do so, greet the fire spirit:

Bright flame, I thank and honour thee, attend to my need today and be the bright sword of my will to sever that which binds (name yourself or person you are helping).

Take your ritual knife in your hands and sit upon the ground to enter a calm visionary state. In your vision, look around yourself or the person you are helping from the outside and "see" the energetic cords binding you, the person, or situation. Go up to each cord and examine it for information; you may gain extra insights into its purpose or where it has come from. Taking great care with the knife and when you are ready, grab hold of the cord with your hand. Pantomiming the physical action, use the knife to "cut" the cord from you about a foot away from your body, seeing in your inner vision how it withers away to nothing. If you sense there is anything left, in your inner vision pull it out and away from you, remembering that nothing has the authority to bind you without your consent, and so such magic against you can only fail when you challenge it. Pull the cord out and cast it either into the fire or the candle flame, where it is instantly destroyed.

Finally, gather your black thread and hold it tight between your two hands. Sitting straight in front of your candle, stare into the flames and pull up plenty of energy into your body. Holding the thread taut, say:

All threads and cords that have tried to bind me have no power here and are severed, never to return!

Repeat as many times as you need, then extend your arms and place the centre of the taut thread over the flame to sever and snap it. Take the rest of the thread and bury it. Flush the salt or throw it away in the dustbin or into a fast-flowing river.

After your ritual, wash thoroughly with a salt scrub.

Practicum
Cord-Cutting to Sever Spirit Attachment

Sometimes the previous ritual is not enough and a troublesome spirit needs to be sent away after their refusal. At such times, especially when using spirit flight or your inner vision, take an iron knife or another iron utensil—a fire poker is perfect for this—and with a sense of the spirit before you, slice the space between you with the iron, saying aloud:

> *I banish you—all connection between us is severed and you may not return! The way is cut with iron!*

You can do this in your inner vision if your hand in the mortal world—the actual, physical room or space—is holding iron. Both are swift and thoroughly effective, so much so that even the threat of iron is sometimes enough to send such unwanted visitors away without further effort.

Fire and Flame

Fire is excellent for breaking hexes, banishing the evil eye, and clearing the energy of all sorts of negative attachments. For this reason, fire and fire-based elementals are frequently used in protection magic. The "need fire" that is ritually created from scratch with a fire striker or a flint and steel is especially powerful in this type of magic.

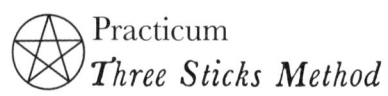

Practicum
Three Sticks Method

If you or someone you are helping has been receiving malicious magic, been crossed (cursed), or is receiving unwelcome visits from spirits, this is a useful technique to remove the crossing placed on you. This tradition shares a lot with the leaping of the Bealtaine fire, which is also used to banish hexes or ill will.

Get a fire suitably roaring with some large sticks and logs outdoors. Select and carefully pull three sticks that are burning at one end from the fire and place them on the ground crossing each other. Taking great care, leap over the sticks safely so that the flame and smoke drive off any energetic attachments from you. When you have leapt over them, douse the flames with freshly drawn water to clear off the ill will and reduce it to nothing.

The Burning Branch

Another method that uses fire to cleanse away ill will and maleficium is traditionally performed at Michaelmas (September 29) or near the equinoxes. This must be performed entirely outdoors. First, light a ritual or need fire from scratch just for this purpose. Take a burning stick or flaming branch, and walk with it clockwise around the outside boundaries of your home or property accompanied by prayers and loud noises to drive off any unwelcome presences. A similar ritual can be created using a candle within the house for blessing the home (see page 91).

Practicum
For Resolving Neighbourly Disputes

To create peace and deflect ill wishes between neighbours, choose a dark night. Take with you a horseshoe and a sprig of St. John's wort, and stand between the two houses at equal distance. Using your inner vision, "see" the threads of dispute flowing between the two households. Taking the horseshoe with its heel upwards, raise your arms and hook the threads, catching them within it and drawing them all together down to the ground. Bury the horseshoe at this place under the earth to deflect the ill will sent between them, wishing that no single household's harm or ill will affect the other. Take the St. John's wort and say:

Herb of St. John, may there be peace and no harm between these two here!

Bury the St. John's wort with the horseshoe. If you can grow a little St. John's wort plant on this spot hereafter, all the better.

Spirit Traps

Glass fishing weights and other glass spheres like Christmas baubles have a long magical history. Sometimes they're filled with tangles of thread or wool to act as spirit traps, the idea being that the unwelcome spirit is attracted to the shiny glass surface and drawn in and trapped by the endlessly tangling thread within. Sometimes the sphere is filled with pins or brightly coloured beads for the same trapping purpose. Protective witch bottles sometimes work in a similar way, though their use and production for protection is described later.

Saining and Glanadh

Saining is a Scots Gaelic practice in which a space is purified and blessed or consecrated, usually with herbal smoke but water and other substances are also used.[13] Early traditional saining rituals from the Isle of Skye tell us that once or twice a year, a house would be ritually cleansed by closing all the windows and doors and burning juniper branches within it until the whole house would be full of smoke. Only then would the doors and windows be opened to let the smoke out. Today this may be impractical, due to the effects of the smoke and the fire risk, but it can easily be adapted into burning herb bundles, made of juniper or other protective aromatic herbs, or using them as incense, with ritual use.

The practice of using herbal smoke for healing and ritual purposes is very ancient and has always had an element of common sense to how it is applied in varying situations. A small amount of incense burnt inside a modern home may be a better idea than the large ritual fires which were historically common in Scotland and Ireland, particularly at Bealtaine and Midsummer/St. John's Eve but the energetic pattern and magical intentions may be the same. It was common at these times, in centuries past, to light two large ritual fires, sometimes of oak, but other suitable magical and medicinal trees and herbs, like rowan, juniper, and hawthorn, were likely also added. These two fires were close enough together for the cattle and the village folk to go in between them and be ritually cleansed by the fire and smoke, and later, when appropriately safe, or when using smaller fires, the flames would be leapt over by the young men and others seeking blessing as part of the Bealtaine celebrations. Children would also be handed over the suitably low flames for healing and protection.

---

13. David Ross and Gavin D. Smith, "Saining," *Scots-English/English-Scots Dictionary* (Hippocrene Books, 1998), 102.

The Irish term *glanadh* (pronounced "glanna") refers to cleansing or clearing.[14] It has many modern day uses and is not overtly a ritual or magical term, but it certainly had ritualistic applications in the past. While there isn't a specific term like "saining" in Irish surviving materials, we do know from the examples above that smoke and fire were used in a cleansing context. For that reason, I present the term here as a Gaelic folk magic alternative to the often inappropriately used "smudging" in reference to burning white sage smudge bundles from Native American practice.

We can perform a saining or glanadh to ritually cleanse our space with fire and smoke, adapting and updating within the traditions to find something powerful and appropriate for us today. Although I like to use these terms because they reflect my heritage, their respectful use is open to anyone. The history of smoke cleansing is universal; this is simply how I do it using herbs and woods that grow in my part of the world and can be ethically sourced.

Practicum
A Ritual House Cleansing with Smoke

Prepare a central candle and another that you can take around the home in a suitably practical holder. Also gather a small mirror, a bowl of spring water or other blessed water, and prepared herbs for burning, again making sure they are in a sensible container—a smoking herb bundle will need a receptacle for falling ash and a ritual fan; to burn loose herbs requires a charcoal brick and a heatproof dish. Don't use incense sticks for this; they won't be pure enough.

Check first that all the house's doors and windows are shut but the cupboards and drawers are open. Next, draw a caim or circle about the house. Go around calling in your power for the work and then light your central candle. From that, light your travelling candle. Carry it with you as you work your way around the house in a clockwise direction, starting at the part of the house furthest from the front or back doors. Make sure the light gets into every corner and nook or cranny of the house. If you need to reflect the light in awkward areas, use the handheld mirror. Go around every doorway and

---

14. "Glan," Foclóir.ie, accessed February 27, 2024, https://www.foclóir.ie/en/dictionary/ei/glan.

window with special care, and in your inner vision take heed of any intrusions you feel, seeing yourself and the light sweeping them towards the front door. Move around the space in such a way to prevent them from being able to get around you, herding them systematically out of the house.

When you have gone all the way around the house with the candle, it's time to burn the incense or herb bundle and repeat the exercise in the same way, seeing that the smoke gets into every corner of the home.

Finally, repeat the same with the blessed water, asserting that the house is blessed as you go around. Complete the rite by opening the doors and sweeping, smoking or flicking water at the open doors leaving space for the unwelcome spirits or energies to go past you out of the house. Open the windows to let any smoke out *only* when the whole house is cleansed.

The charms I like to use for this manner of house cleansing and blessing call upon Brigit, whom I call upon a lot in my practice. I repeat them over and over to build energy when working in this way and adapt them at need. Here are versions I use most.

> *Brigit bless and protect this house*
> *From site to stay*
> *From beam to wall*
> *From end to end*
> *From ridge to basement*
> *From balk to roof tree*
> *From found to summit*
> *Brigit bless and protect this house.*[15]
>
> *This house and all good souls within*
> *Are under the shielding*
> *Of good Brigit each day*
> *This house and all good souls within*
> *Are under the shielding of Brigit each night*
> *Each early and late*

---
15. Adaptation from "Invocation 45, Blessing a House," in Carmichael, *Carmina Gadelica*, 63.

Every dark
And every night.[16]

Poltergeists, Ley Lines, and Fairy Roads

Sometimes household disturbances are a result of natural spirit behaviours and the flow of energy in the local environment, such as rivers and streams as well as the energetic flows of fairy or corpse roads and ley lines around the area. Sometimes, such paths go through a house, and these kinds of dwellings attract stuck and unwelcome spirits in addition to so-called restless spirits. They're also a magnet for other strange behaviours such as random poltergeist activity, things going missing and moving on their own, bad dreams, recurring illness, and the like. Often if the cause is a natural thing, something can be done to alleviate the worst of the effects.

If you are sure a current of earth energy or water flow is the problem, start by tuning in to these presences perhaps using dowsing or spirit work. Then simply seek to befriend and appease these presences with offerings and ask if the flow can be shifted only slightly so that it goes around rather than through the house.

One cottage that I worked with was beset by strange energies and spirit visitations—no sooner had one spirit been passed on to their awaiting ancestors than more arrived as if on a conveyor belt. It was relentless, and unless something was done, this place would never be a peaceful home for long. So, I spoke to the land and learnt that there was a fairy road passing through the edge of the whole row of cottages, right through where the householders slept! Over a short period of time, the spirits of the land there agreed to shift the road ever so slightly so that it ran alongside the house rather than passing through. The spirits were propitiated with offerings of the local crop and allowed all parties to be at peace. Together the spirits and I created a small set of dolmen arches much like one finds at the entrance of a British Neolithic long barrow, only ours was made of small stones to mark the newly adjusted road's path through the garden. That way, the spirits could pass along and make the garden a place for honouring them and leaving gifts and

---

16. Adaptation from "Invocation 264, Blessing of Brigit," in Carmichael, *Carmina Gadelica*, 239.

offerings. There has been peace there ever since, although the way will need to be maintained and respected by the humans to remain.

Hag Stone and Iron

To protect your doorways, get a hag stone and tie it to your door key. One variation of this practice is to tie it with red thread to an old large iron key—keys to a church door are often considered the best for this. Hag stones are powerfully protective in blocking ill will and guard boundaries, just as they are conversely powerful in helping us see spirits. Red thread is as equally powerful in its protective powers as iron, though ensure any thread used is natural—cotton or wool, not plastic or nylon. Tying a hag stone to your housekey casts its protection over all your boundaries, but it may be less practical than crafting a hag stone and key charm you can hang by your door.

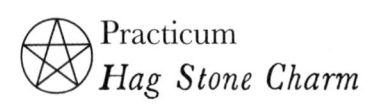

Practicum
Hag Stone Charm

Gather a natural hag stone, an old iron key, and a length of red thread. Bind the stone and key together with the thread, repeating the following charm as you tie three knots in the binding.

> *Red thread, red thread*
> *Put all ill will to fled*
> *Lock and close and guard the door*
> *Protect this house from all and more*
> *Stone and iron and red*
> *Stone and iron and red*
> *Stone and iron and red.*

Repeat the charm over and over until you have either tied the thread three times or until you feel the process of empowering the charm is finished and complete.

Hang the hag stone and key on a hook by the side of your front or back door. You could place one at every boundary if you felt it was needed, but a single well-made charm should be sufficient in most circumstances.

A hag stone can also be threaded on a cord and hung by the door or fireplace for their protection, and it's common to see several hag stones hung together for this purpose. A hag stone hung from a baby's cot or child's bed is powerfully protective, especially when combined with rowan to ensure the child is safe from spirits and bad dreams.

Practicum
Rowan and Red Thread

Another traditional protection charm for a house, person, or property makes use of rowan wood and red thread. There is a great deal of magical lore about the rowan tree; often its magic seems to lie in its ability to see danger before it comes, and it has associations with the colour red from its berries.

Gather two rowan sticks of equal length (about three inches is fine, but bigger or smaller also works). Traditionally the most powerful time to gather rowan wood is at Bealtaine (May 1), but this can be done at any time. I like to gather fallen wood and ask the tree spirit to lend their power to my spell by spending a few moments breathing with the tree and just asking it aloud. This gesture shows my respect and kinship with the tree rather than an attempt to dominate by cutting. Unless I feel a strong *no*, I'm good to go.

Cross the two sticks at right angles to each other and bind with red embroidery thread so that they form an equal-armed cross. Then say:

Rowan and red thread
Keep all ill wishes from this place.[17]

Repeat the words until you have completely tied the thread and sense you are done.

Hang your rowan crosses at the doors and boundaries; they can also be placed under the pillow or beneath the mattress of a cot or child's bed to protect against spirits and ill wishes.

---

17. These are my words, but there are lots of variations of this charm. Another example can be found in Robert Chambers, *Popular Rhymes of Scotland* (W & R Chambers, 1870), 328. For more on the rowan and the magical qualities of trees, see *Celtic Tree Magic* (Llewellyn Publications, 2014).

⛤ Practicum
Saining Charm for Protection

Burning blessing herbs, walk sunwise around the person, chanting:

> *The sain put by Brigit upon her son*
> *Sain from death, sain from wound*
> *Sain from breast, sain from knee*
> *Sain from knee to foot*
> *Sain of the three sains*
> *Sain of the seven sains*
> *From the crown of thy head*
> *To the soles of thy feet.*
> *Sain of the seven fathers, one*
> *Sain of the seven fathers, two*
> *Sain of the seven fathers, three*
> *Sain of the seven fathers, four*
> *Sain of the seven fathers, five*
> *Sain of the seven fathers, six*
> *Sain of the seven fathers, seven*
> *Upon thee now*
> *From the edge of thy brow*
> *To thy coloured soles*
> *To preserve thee from behind*
> *To sustain thee in front*
> *By east or west, west or east,*
> *North or south, south or north!*[18]

---

18. My adaptation from "137, Sain Charm" found in Carmichael, *Carmina Gadelica*, 134–35. I have adapted this from seven paters to calling in the protection of seven ancestral fathers. These need not refer to direct or recent ancestors—they can refer to good spirits who choose to attend to the person's protection.

Practicum
A Charm to Banish the Evil Eye Set Upon Someone

For this charm, you will need a coil of black thread (biodegradable only) and a pair of scissors. Thread in hand, loosely wrap and drape it around the afflicted person. See in your inner vision how it catches and snares the ill will sent towards them. Taking up one end, gather it slowly in an anticlockwise direction, saying the following charm:

I trample upon the eye
As tramples the duck upon the lake
As tramples the swan upon the water
As tramples the horse upon the plain
As tramples the cow upon the field
As tramples the host of the elements!
Power of the wind I have over it
Power of wrath I have over it
Power of fire I have over it
Power of thunder I have over it
Power of lightning I have over it
Power of storms I have over it
Power of moon I have over it
Power of sun I have over it
Power of stars I have over it
Power of the heavens and the worlds
I have over it!

Cast the thread on the ground and stamp on it. Scrunch it up and take the scissors to cut the clump into four pieces, being careful that none of it is lost.

Divide the threads into four clumps, saying:

A portion of it upon the grey stones
A portion of it upon the steep hills

A portion of it upon the fair meads
And a portion of it upon the grey salt sea![19]

Take care to scatter the four clumps far from each other, buried in the earth or thrown into rivers and the sea.

Magical Ashes

Hearth ashes or magical ashes are a powerfully protective magical material, the result of the alchemical magic of the fire and whatever has been burnt in it. Special ashes can be made by intentionally burning special magical woods and herbs for specific aims, such as rowan for protection, apple-wood for love, and so on. Equally, the ash from fires burnt at the full moon, Samhain or Bealtaine or from handfastings or rites of passage all have magical properties.

I keep a special jar to which I add ashes from special fires; when lighting a new magical fire, I add a sprinkle of those magical ashes. In this way, the fire spirits and spirits involved in the working can blend together and grow in power.

I also sometimes keep jars of other ashes that I wouldn't want to add to the main mix—ash from burned ancestral items, for example—that I would want to keep anyway perhaps for future workings or as standalone magical items.

Wood is easy enough to burn to ash, requiring only a little skill and common sense, but burning herbs and more fragile things to ash is easier said than done; care must be taken lest a fire burn the herbs to nothing. For these I use a special pan just for this task or a metal tin with a lid punctured with a small hole. You can place the herbs in the pan or tin with the lid on over the heat of a fire so that the ashes remain inside. In fact, charcoal is made using a similar process.

Soot

Charged and consecrated soot from a hearth is protective and ties directly into the home and hearth's spirit presences and powers, so much so that soot

---

19. My adaptation, from "141, Exorcism of the Eye" from Carmichael, *Carmina Gadelica*, 138.

from another's hearth may be used against them like hair or fingernails, it is deeply personal.

When cold, soot or ashes from your hearth can be used as a protective substance. When mixed with water or other liquids such as alcohol, spring water, or urine, the solution can be used to make an ink for the drawing of protective sigils to repel ill will. Soot is thought to act like a magical "charcoal filter" that blocks toxic energy from entering the home. Bowls of soot can have protective herbs added to draw up negative energy, illness, or distress from a space. Sooty streaks from the putting out of lit tapers have been found around protective witch marks (see the next section) in old houses and stately homes, seeming to suggest this was once considered effective protection against fire.

Witch's Marks

These are protective apotropaic designs usually scratched or carved into walls or other solid materials, usually found in very old homes, barns, and sometimes churches. They come in various forms but I have found all of them to be quite effective; as they draw on centuries of magical use, they have gained a power all their own.

The daisy wheel or hexafoil looks like a six-petaled flower in a circle that is often made with a compass. A single or sometimes a series of overlapping daisy wheels are found across the United Kingdom carved into walls, windowsills, doorways, and fireplaces. They have even been found carved into furniture—really, they were placed anywhere where spirits were thought to find entrance. It is thought that a passing spirit sees a daisy wheel and gets trapped within it.

The daisy wheel is a very old symbol and can be seen in looser form in the rock art found at Loughcrew cairns in County Meath in Ireland, most notably Cairn T, which is illuminated by the equinox sunrise, hinting at its part of a very ancient magic that is now only partially understood.

Overlapping Vs are another type of witch mark commonly found in the United Kingdom and are thought to be Catholic in origin, standing for *Virgo Virginum*, "virgin of virgins," a reference to the Virgin Mary. This is a symbolically feminine design with a power of its own; like much folk magic, it draws from many sources and mixes beliefs. The focus is purely on effectiveness rather than theology.

Illustration 4: Witch Marks Daisy Wheel and VV

⛧ Practicum
A Written Protection Spell for the Home

Write with red ink upon fresh paper (or better still, parchment):

> *Sun, Moon, Mars, Mercury, Jupiter, Venus, Saturn, trine, sextile, dragons head, dragons' tail, I charge you to guard this house from all evils whatsoever, and guard it from all disorders, and from anything being taken wrongly, and give this family good health and wealth!*[20]

---

20. John Harland, *Lancashire Folklore*, (Frederick Warne & Co, 1882), 62. Online edition from Project Gutenberg, accessed June 7, 2024, https://www.gutenberg.org/files/41148/41148-h/41148-h.htm#Page_62.

Place the spell in a small box or pouch and place it over the front door. You may add protective herbs to the box or pouch as well. Remember to renew the spell yearly if not every few months.

Garlic

Garlic is an excellent protective plant, and all parts of it are useful in protection magic. Garlic has lunar correspondences, so this charm is best carried out at the full moon with your own freshly pulled garlic, though it can be adapted as needed.

Practicum
Garlic Charm[21]

Take three or nine bulbs of garlic, and with a large needle or thin nail, pierce through each one, stringing white cord through each bulb and knotting it with this spoken charm:

> *Garlic, as I bind you so you shall bind all harm away from me and this place!*

After the knot has been made, thread the cord through the next bulb and so on until they are knotted as one string.

Hang the string at your household's boundaries and replace after three or nine months or when the garlic begins to rot. As the garlic rots or dries, so will any ill will sent towards you. After, bury the bulbs in the earth; should they take root, do not eat or use them. Instead, place them to grow at the boundaries or four corners of the property.

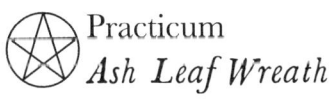

Practicum
Ash Leaf Wreath

This charm is as good for protection as it is for staying ill-spoken words and gossip against you as well as preventing slander or secret telling. It makes use of the ash tree's magical protectiveness against the viper, adder, and all metaphorical venoms.

---

21. A different historical version of this can be seen at the Museum of Witchcraft and Magic, Boscastle. "Charm, Garlic," accessed February 27, 2024, https://museumofwitchcraftandmagic.co.uk/object/charm-garlic.

After some time communing with the ash tree, gather some of the leaves into a bunch. Bind it together with red thread, and hang it at the windows or the hearth. In my county of Somerset, it is often made into a wreath and hung at the front door on the outside or hung from the nearest tree or gatepost.

Bunches of ash keys—their winged seed heads—are also good boundary protectors.

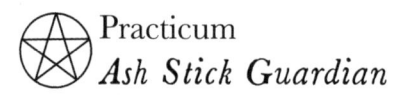

⛤ Practicum
Ash Stick Guardian

After communion with the tree and its spirit, cut or find a fallen ash branch three to five feet in length. Carve or scratch upon its surface two eyes. If it has knots or twigs to cut off, paint or carve eyes there as well. You may peel the bark off with a knife along its whole or just the areas where you carve or scratch the eye designs. Rub linseed oil into any areas that have been stripped. Take a little cayenne pepper, ochre, or red paint, and redden the eyes with this protective colour.

Spend a day and a night with your ash stick, honouring it as a friend. In spirit flight or inner vision, seek its name or grant it one in honour.

Place the stick by the front door as a guardian. Speak to it often, greeting it when you return home. See that it is in a stable position where it can stay undisturbed. Should it ever fall, know that it is telling you trouble or unwelcome visitors is coming. At such times or when you need extra care or shelter, place the stick across the door to bar the way.

Witch Bottles

Traditional witch bottles are apotropaic items that protect the home and its occupants from maleficium—hexes, crossing, and the evil eye. The earliest known bottles in Britain date back to the 1600s, but they remained similar in their construction until the twentieth century.[22] There were numerous ways in which they were made and used, but the contents most commonly used were iron nails and urine.

---

22. Brian Hoggard, *Magical House Protection: The Archaeology of Counter-Witchcraft* (Berghann Books, 2021), 32.

Urine has a long history in European and Celtic folk magic—one traditional ward to stop ghosts and other spirits from entering the house is to urinate upon the boundaries. Bodily fluids seem to be territorial in their magical function as well as a repellent, hence the use of spittle as a hex breaker. Another use of urine in a witch bottle is in the formation of a spirit trap that fools the spirits into thinking it is the person they intend to harm as well as in a form of sympathetic magic, particularly if one of the forms of maleficia appears to be illness or bladder infection.

Sometimes the urine is kept in a bottle with other apotropaic items, but at other times it was boiled in an iron pan to which nails and pins were added. The brew would be left to boil until it was evaporated or the person who sent the attack was identified. Some accounts mention adding an animal's heart punctured with pins, but this practice was later adapted into a cloth heart into which pins were stuck. Adding the heart was said to make the malicious magic reflect and rebound to the person who sent it, resulting in them having terrible stomach pains and the sensation of burning urine until they removed the spell. Such methods were commonly used to identify witches who were said to cry out for the boiling to stop, thus identifying themselves.

In other accounts, the urine was poured into large clay salt-glazed jugs. The most popular design of pottery jug was one with a bearded male face upon it in decoration called Bellarmines, named after the seventeenth-century Italian cardinal Robert Bellarmine, whose likeness it was intended to capture. Bent iron nails were placed in these jugs; the bending of metal items for magical use itself a practice that dates back to Bronze Age British Isles where bent bronze swords would be placed in rivers and marshes as offerings. It was thought that by putting these items out of action in this world by bending them, the items were given life and power in the next world. The iron and its shape as a weapon were believed to return any malicious magic sent to the inhabitants whilst also entrapping malicious spirits sent to the house.

Other items were also added to the witch bottle to add more protection and deflecting abilities. These items typically included but were not limited to animal hearts, discussed earlier (a practice I strongly discourage—these were later substituted with cloth hearts), teeth, small animal bones, keys, written charms, fingernails, broken glass, thorns from blackthorn trees, salt, soot, brick dust, tangles of thread, or what were known as binding cords: knotted rope or cord used in binding spells. While historically we don't know what spell was bound in these cords, it's likely that they were spells to literally bind the urine of the attacking witch or bind and prevent them from doing the household harm. It's also possible they were used to bind prayers into the bottle such as repeating protective psalms as the cord was knotted, once per repetition.

Later examples of this tradition continue well into the twentieth century with more modern bottles being used, sometimes sealed with wax and/or the cork stuck with pins. And even more recently, as magical practices have become revived, witch bottles may contain vinegar or wine instead of urine. It could be an indication of modern concerns of squeamishness on the part of modern practitioners; urine is still perhaps the most potent ingredient a practitioner can use, but these bottles are only suitable if the person making them is also the householder using them. When a practitioner makes a witch bottle for others, using vinegar may be easier than asking the person being helped to provide their own ingredients!

Practicum
A Simple Modern Witch Bottle Formula

Take a dark glass bottle or clay bottle that has never been used before. To it add either your own urine or that of the biggest or strongest person in the house. If you prefer, substitute vinegar. Into this bottle, add nine old bent nails. As you add each nail, say:

As you seek to harm me/us, so the harm is done only to yourself.

Next, add your nail clippings and those from every person in the house so that the protection covers each of you. As you add the clippings, say:

I am [or name of person] and this house are protected now.

You may decide you don't want any physical items from a person in it, in which case items such as glass shards (be careful), a tangle of black thread, salt, soot, or any other suitable ingredients can be added.

After sealing the bottle or jar with red or black wax, place it somewhere it will never be disturbed or seen: under the floorboards, behind the hearth, or in the roof beams were all traditional spots, but every home has always adapted how this is done through the centuries, and you are no exception!

Practicum
Other Witch Bottle Formulas

The modern practice of using witch bottles has evolved hugely, and often these formulas work quite well even if their focus is slightly different. You may therefore find a formula for house protection that includes vinegar, salt, tangled thread, and protective herbs such as sprigs of rosemary and blackthorn or chopped pieces of bramble.

If you are certain who is psychically attacking you or sending malicious spirits your way, you could always write their name on a piece of paper and stick two pins through it in an X shape, saying as you do so:

You have no power over me, (insert their name here), and can do me no harm.

Place the paper in the bottle and seal it with wax. Bury it at the perimeter of your property. I like this version as it means that you are not harming the other person—only stopping them from harming you. It allows for error in case the issue is really coming from elsewhere.

Chapter 6
A Witch's Wheel of the Seasons

The ever-turning seasons are a source of constant support and education to the folk magic practitioner. As they are living examples of change and renewal, alignment with nature's rhythms is a spiritual guide all in itself that also magically creates a potent source of power for transformation that can be used in a thousand ways as the moon waxes and wanes and the green world rotates from winter to summer and back again. We may notice how, like nature, we are continually on the edge of change. We find opportunities in the liminal spaces between the high days of summer and winter when, like the natural world itself, we are never all one thing but instead carry onwards momentum that can just as easily block as it can encourage us along the paths we take in this life.

Whether we embrace the natural rhythms of nature or strive to leave them behind, their power over us is unavoidable. But if we work with them and align our work with the flow of the great seasonal currents, we find more power and it may sometimes seem as if the world itself supports our magics.

Today we think of the Wheel of the Year as eight seasonal festivals: the winter and summer solstices; the autumn and spring equinoxes; and the four so-called Celtic fire festivals positioned equidistant between them—Imbolc, Bealtaine, Lughnasadh, and Samhain. However, while these festivals all have long histories, placing them all together in a system in this way is a relatively modern thing. In times past, not all areas of the Celtic lands and Britain honoured all of these festivals, and what and how they marked their seasonal calendars varied geographically. There are also numerous lesser-known festivals of local importance with rich regional variations. When we work with the powers of place in our own locations, these local festivals can be very potent sources of power indeed. The wheel of the seasons is a vast subject, and there are a great many resources available to assist the practitioner in honouring them. The following gives a brief summary of the seasonal festivals and some key ways to honour them.

Winter Solstice: Approximately December 21

The winter solstice marks the shortest day and the longest night, when the sun reaches its most southerly position along the horizon before gradually rising a little further north day after day until the summer solstice.

Many ancient neolithic monuments are aligned to the winter solstice sunset/summer solstice sunrise axis, showing us that thousands of years ago, this event was important. During the solstice, the sun appears to stand still on this position upon the horizon each dawn from a few days before until around the December 25, when its journey north is evident enough to be seen with the naked eye once again, suggesting rebirth.

Winter rituals and rites for the solstice are entwined with those of Christmas and Yule but essentially revolve around a period of rest and endings before the sun's renewal.

Greeting the dawn or the sunset at winter solstice is a powerful and moving thing to do, especially if you are able to visit an ancient site aligned to the winter solstice sun. As the sun rises, see it filling you with light and renewal; as it sets, see it taking with it everything in your life you no longer need or is holding you back. Sending blessings to the dead at this time is also effective, and encouraging any trapped spirits to find their release on the midwinter sunset is highly effective.

Twelfth Night Wassail: January 5 or 6

Wassail is the custom of blessing the apple trees of the orchard to scare away any evil spirits and to "wake" them to provide abundance in the coming year. It can take many forms with all sorts of local variations, but loosely it involves making a great sound to scare away the evil spirits—sometimes with a gunshot or with roaring or whooping. Sometimes an arrow is shot into the trees again to scare away the spirits but also perhaps symbolic of the returning sun. The trees are then hung with toast, and warm spiced cider is poured at their roots as an offering. Following this is usually singing, particularly of the numerous versions of the wassail song and general merriment.

These days in Somerset, a shotgun is usually deployed as part of the ritual, and it is striking to see the sparks and smoke of the shot rising up into the air on a cold winter's night. There's always great jubilation at the sudden shock of energetic release that comes from its loud bang.

The word "wassail" comes from the Saxon *Waes hael*, or "be in good health," which is cried aloud at the receiving of the wassail drink. There are numerous wassail recipes for spiced mead or cider that serves as the communal drink served usually from a large wassail bowl that no doubt has antecedents in the large communal feasting cauldrons of the Celtic past.

Somerset Apple Tree Wassail Song

Old apple tree
We'll wassail thee
And hoping thou wilt bear;
The lord does know
Where we shall be
To be merry another year.
To blow well
And to bear well
And so merry let us be
Let every man drink up his cup
And health to the old apple tree![23]

---

23. Traditional folk song, found in Cecil Sharp (ed. and comp.), *Folk Songs from Somerset* (Simpkin & Co., the Wessex Press, 1904), https://archive.org/details/imslp-songs-from-somerset-sharp-cecil/SIBLEY1802.5603.14249.2bee- 39087013594496fifthseries/page/n83/mode/2up?q=somerset.

Imbolc: February 1

Imbolc means "in the belly" in Irish, and refers to the time of year when the lambs begin to birth (sometimes it is known as *Oimelc*, a term that related to ewe's milk) and the first green shoots of the coming spring become visible. Traditionally this holiday is associated with the goddess Brigit, a goddess of fire and fertility in the form of dairy, produce, and domestic care. She is also a goddess of poetry and creativity as well as smithcraft. The old tales of this time of year often describe her ritual battle with (or her transformation from) the Cailleach of winter to the youthful Brigit who brings springtime and life back to the land.

Imbolc is one of the cross-quarter days or fire festivals stationed equidistantly between the solstices and equinoxes. It is of particular importance in Ireland and Scotland, where a great many celebrations and ritual acts accompany this time of year to honour the saint and goddess Brigit and bring protection into the home.

One custom good for folk healing practices is to prepare the *brat bride*, or Brigit's cloak, a piece of cloth or a small blanket traditionally coloured red or white. Brigit's cloak is hung on a bush outside overnight on the eve of Imbolc to gather Brigit's blessing when she passes, bringing the spring. The cloak is used when someone is ill, placed on their bed or when laving them with spring water when they are fevered. It can also be used to comfort those in distress and has been known to inspire healers regarding what the patient needs and in getting an accurate diagnosis.

Spring Equinox: Approximately March 21

Like the autumn equinox, the spring equinox is found marked in the alignments of our most ancient archaeological sites, hinting that both were once events of great ritual significance. These days it is associated with the Saxon festival of Ostara, whose name is drawn from Eos, the Proto-Germanic goddess of the dawn, suitable for the dawning of the agricultural year when it finally becomes warm enough to sow seeds and work outdoors with some regularity. *Equinox* means "equal night," referring to the fact that the day and night are of equal length.

The spring equinox is a good time for planting and sowing magical herbs as well as for preparing the witch's garden for the growing year.

St. Mark's Eve: April 24

Although there are many folk traditions about St. Mark's Eve, one of the main ones describes it as a key time for seeing who will die over the coming year.

Traditionally one goes alone and in silence to sit in the porch of the village church just before the clock strikes midnight. As midnight comes, so shall the spirits of the dead and the shades of those soon to die. They proceed through the churchyard or past those sitting into the church. The living must not say anything to them nor look them in the eye as they pass.

Another practice local to me in the southwest is to go to the churchyard at midnight and take three tufts of grass from the churchyard, carry it home in a white cloth, and place it under the pillow, repeating three times:

The eve of Saint Mark by prediction is blest
Set therefore my hopes and fears all to rest
Let me know my fate whether weal or woe
Whether my rank be high or low
Whether to be single or whether a bride
And the destiny my star does provide![24]

Bealtaine: May 1

Bealtaine marks the first day of summer in folkloric tradition, although in practice it may feel more like the height of spring in northern Europe. This is another Celtic fire festival and cross-quarter day, but there are numerous ways the true day of Bealtaine may be calculated. The main one is the day when the hawthorns blossom, another is determined by its astrological dating, when the Sun reaches the midpoint of 15 degrees in Taurus, making it more like May 4 or 5 (although this changes slightly year to year).

---

24. Sarah Hewett, *Nummits and Crummits: Devonshire Customs, Characteristics and Folk-Lore* (Forgotten Books, 2020), 33. Originally published 1900 by Thomas Burleigh.

This time is said to be especially potent for fairy contact and was historically seen as a time of great revelry but also danger, as it is one of the key "spirit nights" of the year.

Ritual fires should be lit outside at Bealtaine, and we seek their blessing and purification by leaping over their flames when the fire has burned low enough. Spells for sexuality, healing, the fertility of the land, and connecting with the spirits on the land are powerful at this time as well.

Summer Solstice and Midsummer: Approximately June 21 and June 25

The summer solstice is of course the mirror of the winter solstice; it is the longest day and the shortest night when the sun rises at its most northerly point along the horizon (due northeast) before visually appearing to pause and then gradually travelling a little further south again each dawn until winter.

The summer solstice is marked at several stone circles and other neolithic monuments, most notably Stonehenge. This is a time to feel the height of your power and success in the world and to fill yourself up with lifeforce. Midsummer is the day when the sun is seen to rise a little further south again, usually June 25.

Now is the time to revel in an outdoor life and forage for wild foods and magical or medicinal herbs. It is also the perfect time to align with the solar forces and charge up yourself and your staff with the earth's serpent currents via long rambles across the land and overnight vigils at places of power.

Lughnasadh: August 1

Lughnasadh is the first of the harvest festivals, when the crops in the fields are growing golden and ripe. At this time, we honour the earth and her generosity.

Lughnasadh means "the funerary games of Lugh," an Irish god probably cognate with the Celtic Lugos. In the literary traditions of Ireland, Lugh held funerary games on this day for his stepmother, Tailtiu, who cleared the plains of Ireland so they could be used for crops but died in the process. In this tale we see the honouring of the transition from the hunter-gatherer's wild land to the farmer's cultivated land, serving as a reminder that the earth makes a great sacrifice for our way of life. Another name for this time is *Brón Trogain*, which means the "sorrows of the earth," suggesting its suffering to give us the life we wish for.[25]

The Anglo-Saxon name for this time is *Lammas* ("loaf mass"), a reference to the ripening crops of barley and wheat used to make bread at this time.

Autumn Equinox: Approximately September 21

Like the spring equinox, the autumn equinox is when day and night are of equal length before it tips over into the dark half of the year towards winter and the winter solstice. This is a prime harvest festival where many wild foods and berries may be foraged and the vegetable garden reaches its peak. At this time, much food must be stored and prepared for the winter.

Now is the time to practice gratitude and to thank the earth spirits for their abundance and generosity.

Michaelmas: September 29

It could well be that many of the earlier rituals and lore around the autumn equinox were moved to Michaelmas in the Christian period, but this day is still potent in Celtic folk magic. In Scotland in particular, rituals of cleansing and warding are done at this time together with harvest blessing.

Michaelmas is a good time to beat the bounds around your home or community. It was traditional to draw a caim around the house or other property (sometimes the church) at this time while carrying flaming torches. This practice can of course be performed today around any space with candles and incense, or even hag torches (torches made from dried mullien stalks or other flammable material).

Another tradition states that it is taboo to pick blackberries after this date—after September 29, they belong to the devil!

---

25. We find the term *Brón Trogain* in the Irish text *Acallamh na Senórach* ("Dialogue of the Ancients") as well as in the *Tochmarc Emire* ("The Wooing of Emer"). Maire Mac Neill suggests its meaning—"the earth suffers under its fruits" is a metaphor based on "the travail of birth." *The Festival of Lughnasa: A Study of the Celtic Festival of the Beginning of the Harvest* (University College Dublin, 2008), 10–11.

Samhain: October 31

The final harvest festival of the year, Samhain is a time for honouring the dead and the chthonic forces in life, those elements of the spirit world and our fate and destiny that are impossible to control. It is perhaps the most powerful spirit night of the year and is highly potent for magic and spirit contact.

It is traditional at this time to honour the dead and the ancestors, and to use scrying or divination to gain insight into the year ahead. It is also important at Samhain to renew any protection around the house and home.

Illustration 5: Carved Tumpshie or Mangelwurzel

Punkie Night: Last Thursday of October

Punkie night is a regional Somerset version of Samhain, usually held the last Thursday of October, although now it aligns more closely with Samhain/Halloween as the tradition is being revived. At punkie night, carved mangel-wurzels are made into lanterns much like the traditional carved turnips or tumpshies and the later American pumpkins. In an echo of trick-or-treat traditions, children knock on doors asking for candles with the following song:

Give me a candle, give me light
If you haven't a candle, a penny's all right [26]

The term "punkie" is clearly drawn from the old Celtic names for troublesome spirits, notably the Cornish *Bucca* and its relatives the Welsh *Pwca* and the Irish *Púca*. Punkie is also known as "picwinnie" in Somerset and may have once been related to fishing or sea spirits.

---

26. Jacqueline Simpson and Steve Roud, "Punkie Night," in *Oxford Dictionary of English Folklore* (Oxford University Press, 2003), 287.

Chapter 7
Moon Magic

Any magic made in relation to nature and her rhythms must pay some mind to the turn of the seasons as well as to the turning of day and night and the small chiming times when magic seems to enter the daily mundane world on its own volition. Such times are the gateways of the day, dawn and dusk, high noon and midnight, as well as the tides and cycles of the moon's rotations and its subtle pull on all life, from heaving seas to burrowing earthworms.

Any witch will be aware of the special silvered atmosphere on a clear night at the full of the moon—indeed for many it provides a pull to wander outside and explore the world anew under its subtle light. It has long been what first calls someone to seek magic and spiritual connection. There are some who feel little delight and spare only a passing thought at seeing the moon riding high on a sky filled with stars; these are not folk naturally pulled to magic. It is those who feel their heart rise and filled at the sight who tend to be the ones to push at the borders of the day and the humdrum world in search of something stranger. These are the ones who find magic hidden in the secret places of the world—spirits in doorways, visions at the church porch, voices in the river. These are the ones who find the edges, and these are the ones who truly earn the titles "witch," "wise," and "cunning."

There are hosts of spells and practices related to the moon. Some are handed down through generations. Some are recent, and others have been excavated from the pages of grimoires and the recorded oral testimonies carefully preserved by folklorists. However, without the experiential element, without this call to the edges and really spending time building relationship with the sources of magic that surround us, all these words will be as dry as dust. I urge you to step outside, look up, and explore the skies. Learn to feel their subtle (and not-so-subtle) pulls on our souls to learn some of the magics that go beyond words.

The Movements of the Moon

The moon rotates around the earth every 27.3 days; for most people's purposes, roughly every 28 days. This is called a sidereal month, measured by its position relative to distant, so-called fixed stars. As the moon rotates, it goes at the same pace as its own orbital motion, so it always shows the same face to us from Earth. However, it also goes through phases from new to full to new again, a journey that takes 29.5 days, a synodic month. The difference between the sidereal and synodic month is the result of the moon's movement around Earth, which is also moving around the sun. Therefore, our moon must travel a little further to make up the distance. The dark side of the moon is the side that faces way from Earth and can't be seen unless we are in outer space; in fact, as the moon rotates, this side of the moon sees as much sunlight as the side facing us and has also been mapped during lunar missions. The moon shines due to it reflecting light from the sun, and its shape in the sky changes only due to the movement of light and shadow upon its surface.

The dark of the moon, the new moon, is when the moon's surface is entirely shadowed by the earth so it cannot be seen, gradually appearing as a crescent sliver as the sun's light begins to reach past Earth. As the moon continues its counterclockwise orbit around Earth as seen from the North Pole, more and more of it becomes illuminated by the sun until it reaches the full moon stage and we can see all of the moon reflecting the sun's light.

Between new and full moon, the amount of light reflected on the moon increases from the right to the left side; after this stage, the light decreases or wanes at which time the amount of moon not illuminated grows from right to left. To remember this, imagine that the first sliver of new moon is rather like a capital D without the vertical line, and as the moon wanes the crescent becomes a capital C.

⛤ Practicum
Finding the Flow

See if you can imagine the flow of energy or life force flowing through space from the sun reaching and shining on the moon and in turn being shone on Earth. Spend some time contemplating how this energy is transformed by its reflection on the moon and then down to us. You might like to visualise the shift from fiery golden sunlight to silvery moonlight. When meditating on this, what thoughts or images come to mind? Rather than rationalising them or thinking about the science of it, see if you can feel your way into how the energy flows and changes. Whatever you sense can help you in turn intuit how this energy can be used for magic and spiritual insights.

We may use our awareness of the moon to time and pace our magical and spiritual work and align it with the moon's patterns of growth and decline. All life on Earth is subtly affected by the moon; it affects the ocean's tides and the water in our bodies, and its touch is even felt in the way plants grow. Taking this a little further into working with lunar energy is rather like catching a current in the sea or a tidal shift to carry us to our destination.

Guide to Lunar Cyclical Pattern
New Moon/Waxing Crescent

This is a time of new emerging life and the seed of ideas. It is a powerful time when the energy goes from an inner-focused, underworld-oriented current to one that starts to break free in the outer world of manifestation and action. Things started now have a full two weeks of lunar waxing before the energy begins to recede again.

Waxing Gibbous

Also known as a half-moon, this is where things can become more established and take on some weight and momentum. Here we see subtle changes begun at the new moon become actualised and physical. Imagine the new moon as a seed coming into its first green shoot emerging from its seed husk. The waxing gibbous moon is where the first leaves appear.

Full Moon

This is where the lunar energies are at their strongest. This is a time of great power, but it lies often in stillness rather than in change. Now is the time for meditation and for drawing in the moon's energy to carry you forwards for another month. It is a good time for spellwork, especially magic based on charms or talismans that can be charged with the moon's power. In the Celtic Gaulish Coligny calendar that dates to the second century CE, the full moons are highlighted; it is likely that the Celtic month was delineated full moon to full moon, with each month broken into two parts: two weeks to the full and two weeks past it. The full moon can be considered a time of completion and fruition before the energy begins to wane.

Waning Gibbous

This is another half-moon, this time with the light reducing. This is a time when the energy begins to drain away and a time of change can be felt. This is a good time to focus on things that need to be let go of, transformed, or banished. Let the waning moon reduce the power from whatever you are focusing on and take it back to nothing and darkness.

Waning Crescent

Here we see the crescent moon once more now appearing more like a sickle in the sky, signifying a time of reaping and cutting ties. Now is a good time to cut the energetic threads that attach you to anything unwanted or in need of leaving behind in your life. Here we see the touch of the Cailleach, the winter or crone goddess, the great hag who ushers in death and endings. This is not necessarily a negative time; there is a great sense of release and ease that may come at this time as tensions and things that have built up to uncomfortable levels begin to relax. This is a potent time for earthing and grounding rituals.

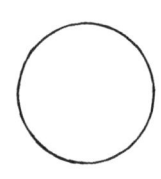

The Dark of the Moon

This is an at-most two-day period before the new moon where it is no longer visible in the night sky. Sometimes it results in very dark nights, but more often it allows the stars in the night sky to become far more visible. For some, there is a tangible sense that the stellar realms are felt more strongly at this time. The dark of the moon is a sacred time when we stand without the moon's guidance on the inner planes and must enter the great cauldron of creation and inspiration if we are to find inner vision and transformation. The Irish Celts once had a ritual for seeking vision called *Imbas Forosnai*, "wisdom that illuminates." The oracular poet or seer would spend time in utter darkness in search of a vision, in a form of sensory deprivation to let the inner eyes see all the clearer. The dark moon provides opportunities for this depth of vision seeking and allows for great treasure to be drawn up from the unseen parts of psyche or from aspects of the spirit world which we are usually unable to reach. This phase is excellent for seeking deep healing, soul and ancestral work, divination, or dream magic.

Practicum
Moon Water

Moon water, sometimes known silver water, is excellent for adding power to spells or cleansing and blessing any space or ritual tool. There are a great many ways it can be made, but the bones of the matter are very simple. Take a bowl that feels suitable (a crystal or clear glass bowl would be ideal) and fill it with fresh spring water. Bottled water will do, but it is best to collect water from a spring or clear river if you are able. If you like, you could place a silver object in the water to add its properties to the potion or add herbs or crystals. If you add the latter, keep it to only one or two items and ensure they are compatible with the subtle lunar energy. Take some time out meditating with the moon, and when you feel ready, raise the bowl up to the moon, and ask her to bless and charge these waters with her sacred energy, so that you can use it for blessing and protection. Take a few deep breaths and let the light of the moon fall upon the water. In your inner vision, see the moon's rays flowing down into the bowl. If the bowl is glass, you may like to see if you can see the moon through the water to add further power and as an act of connection and for seeking an oracular vision.

After a while, lower the bowl and place it somewhere safe outside or on a windowsill where it can continue to receive the moon's rays until dawn.

Before sunrise, remove any materials from the water and carefully bottle it in a dark glass bottle, jar, or some other container used only for this purpose. The water can then be used until the following full moon. Only drink the water or add it to anything that you might consume if the water was fit to drink in the first place *and* if nothing toxic was added in your ritual.

Moon water is effective if sprinkled around the home to bless your space, or added to a purifying bath water to clear off unwanted energies. It can also be used in an oil burner or other evaporator to be released into the air—the possibilities are many and varied.

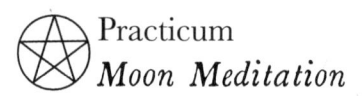

Practicum
Moon Meditation

Try this exercise at full moons, ideally fully in the moonlight. Sitting or standing, place your feet hip-width apart flat on the ground—barefoot is best if it is practical. Lengthen your spine so you are upright, and focus your breathing deep in your belly, slow and calm, letting your thoughts and the memories of the day slip away.

Focus your eyes upon the moon and let yourself place all your attention on its light and its form in the sky. What details can you see on its surface? Become fully present to your place on the land, and your vision of the moon so that it is like a connection, a bond forming between you like a strong silver thread. As you breathe, try to be receptive and in your inner vision, try breathing in the moonlight; as you fill your lungs, see in your inner vision how you pull upon the silver thread and slowly fill your body, mind, and energy field with the light of the moon.

Let your eyes rest gently on the moon, focus softening, maintaining the silver thread and breathing it in. Allow any thoughts or visions to pass through your mind like a silver river.

You may like to stay as you are for some time. If this practice is new for you, you might feel a few minutes is enough but over time and with more practice, you may be able to stay in a lucid connection like this for half an hour or more.

When you feel a strong connection and are able to maintain it for a longer period, you may find you begin to get clearer visions, insights, and messages from the moon that may answer your questions or provide greater insights to your life and what surrounds you, or even sometimes insights to a broader area such as national or even planetary concerns. (Chants and prayers appear at the end of the section, should you wish to use them.)

You could say prayers to the moon or sing chants as acts of gratitude and relationship, or as part of a wider ritual that establishes a trance state. Build up all these skills gently if you are new to this kind of work, knowing that they can be developed quite organically if given time and dedication. You may also like to slowly raise your arms to match the amount of energy and magical charge you feel from the moon until your arms are raised above your head to either side of you. When you do this, see how it feels and adjust the height depending on what feels right at the time. When you have done this a few times, try leaning your upraised arms ahead of you a little as if to embrace the moon and welcome in her energy and silver threads—see how this feels to you.

After a while, it will feel like time to finish the exercise. Lower your arms if you have raised them and let any spare energy sink into the earth. Take care to thank the moon for her assistance and connection and ground yourself well, by stamping your feet and perhaps eating or drinking, and perhaps record your experiences in a journal.

Moon Goddesses

In Britain and Ireland and Celtic traditions generally, there is no specific god or goddess of the moon. In the Welsh tradition is Cerridwen, sacred muse of the bards and most likely once an initiatory goddess of seers and warriors. However, much of her story is also lost, and her role has diminished to the witch in a folktale concerning the rebirth and initiation of the poet magician Taliesin. Cerridwen is associated with her cauldron of Awen or inspiration, and she is in modern times associated with the crescent moon. Her connection with inspiration, magic, and a sacred cauldron seem as if they could have lunar associations, but again the link is implied if we read it that way, rather than overt in any of the original sources.

When we consider the gods and goddesses of the Celts and northern Europe generally, we must understand that we have lost a great deal of knowledge, and what *is* left are only fragments. It is more than possible that there were several lunar divinities now lost to time. Certainly, Iron Age European goddesses featured several associated during the Roman period with Diana, the Roman huntress goddess associated with the moon—the Gaulish forest goddesses Arduinna and Abnoba being the most notable examples. Although we have lost a lot about how they were worshipped, this lunar connection via Diana suggests that if we wish to give a name to a Celtic moon goddess, many good possibilities exist whose connection with the wild, the forest, and hunting we may use to help us tune in to and connect with them.

In my practice, I've always sensed the moon is a woman—her connection to women's menstrual cycles and the classic traditional view of the moon being associated with intuition, psychic abilities, and dreams all feel "feminine" to me. When in deep meditation at the full of the moon, I still instinctively call her "Lady" and resist any firmer title. This fluidity of thinking is typical of moon magic and lunar connection; it relies on something more than the rational mind…and of course who am I to limit the moon or any deity by my own perceptions? There has to be room for what is simply felt and flows organically. As I work with both Cerridwen and Abnoba and connect with the moon through my work with them as well, I allow myself to follow the intuitive flow and let the logical delineations and divisions step aside, accepting that I work in relationship and not by any hard, fast rules; the mystery and the inconsistency work well for me.

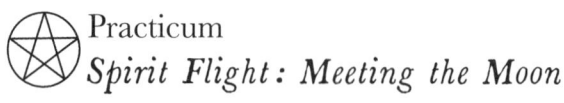

Practicum
Spirit Flight: Meeting the Moon

This exercise will require at least thirty minutes of uninterrupted time as well as a clear space in which to work in your inner vision, leaving room for spirit walking if you can take it deep enough, into a clear connection and dialogue with the moon. You may like to prepare a sacred space: Cast a circle or another preparation, and light a single white candle dedicated to your work with the moon, if you like.

Sit comfortably with your back straight, and let your eyes rest upon the candle flame or, if you can see it, the moon itself. Breathe slow and deep. Let your vision of the room around you begin to fade as you call upon the moon, invoking her and asking that you spend some time with her in spirit. Try this prayer or make your own.

Moon, moon, beautiful moon, fairer far than any star, please bless me with your presence.

See yourself in your inner vision standing on a path of white, chalky earth with green fields on either side of you. Look down at your feet; see them on the ground. Walk along the path to find yourself led through trees and a rich nighttime landscape beneath a deep blue sky filled with stars.

As you walk, you hear the hooting of an owl and glimpse its white shape swoop through the trees overhead and down the path, disappearing into the night.

Next, the path climbs up a smooth slope. The landscape below you opens into rolling fields and forests but ahead climbs higher and higher, weaving through sparse tree cover until you see you are near the top of a high hill. The stars shine brightly around you and seem to be accompanying you as you walk. Through the silvery light you see a hare run ahead of you. You lift your eyes to follow it to the very summit of the hill, where you see the moon is rising and a tall, shimmery, bright figure is waiting for you.

As you draw near, the shape shifts and shivers, changing form over and over, until it finally settles as you approach. Greet the Lady of the Moon as she appears to you at this time, showing your care and respect. Allow plenty of time to receive her wisdom and visions in whatever way they present themselves—each one and her very presence are great gifts.

After some time passes, it will be clear that your audience with the moon is drawing to a close. When you are ready, give her your thanks and love before returning the way you came down the hill. When you reach the bottom, let your breathing and the blood pumping through your heart guide you like a drum back into your body.

When you have come back into your body, take some time to really ground. Wiggle your fingers and toes as you return to your everyday consciousness. You may also like to eat and drink afterwards to feel fully back in your body. Don't forget to record your experience in your journal.

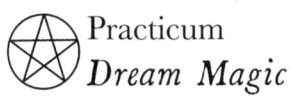

Practicum
Dream Magic

Another way to work with the moon is with dream magic. Dreams at the full or dark moon have extra significance, so it's good to keep a record of your dreams in a dream journal that includes the date and moon phase for later reference.

Before you go to bed, take note of the moon's current phase. If it's full, take a moment to gaze at the full moon and breathe in its silvery light. When you are ready, ask the moon to give you a dream. If the moon is currently dark, ask the night sky.

Prepare an herbal dream tea (such as the mugwort tisane on page 210 to which I'd add lavender), and drink it before settling down. The next morning, record anything you remember from your dream in a journal.

Dream Charm Bags

You can also support your dreamwork with a dream charm bag placed under your pillow. Note: Do not use mugwort if you are pregnant or have menstrual issues.

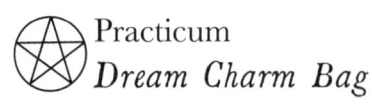

Practicum
Dream Charm Bag

You will need

- 1 white or silver pouch
- 3 spoons dried mugwort
- 3 spoons dried lavender
- 3 spoons dried vervain

Optional
- 3 small white stones. White rolled quartz from the beach is best, but tumbled quartz or moonstone are also suitable

Create a sacred space and gather your materials. Take three deep, calming breaths to prepare, and call upon the moon to assist you in your spell. You might like to use these words or create your own:

Moon, moon beautiful moon, aid me with my magics tonight.
Moon, moon beautiful moon, aid me with my magics tonight.
Moon, moon beautiful moon, aid me with my magics tonight.

The phrase is repeated three times because three is a sacred number to the moon. It could also be repeated up to nine times (3 x 3) to help build our power and intention.

Take each herb one at a time, and breathing slow, thank the spirit of the plant and ask that it aid your magic.

For example:

Spirit of mugwort, hear my prayer, lend your power to my spell. Thank you.

While visualising the light of the moon, gently breathe upon the herb to imbue it with the moon's energy before placing it into the bag.

When each ingredient has been added, hold the bag in your hands and breathe slowly, drawing in the light of the moon and transferring it into the bag in your inner vision. You might like to say your prayer to the moon or chant it aloud for a few minutes to build up your power.

Store the bag in a darkened space—a bedside drawer is great. When you wish to use your charm bag, hold it as you say the prayer again and place it under your pillow.

Illustration 7: Charm Bag

⭐ Practicum
Queen of the Night: A Chant in Honour of the Moon

This traditional chant can be used for all lunar-based magics.

Hail unto thee
Jewel of the night!
Beauty of the heavens
Jewel of the night!
Mother of the stars
Jewel of the night!
Fosterling of the sun
Jewel of the night!
Majesty of the stars
Jewel of the night![27]

---

27. From "312 Queen of the Night" in Carmichael, *Carmina Gadelica*, 289.

Practicum
A New Moon Lunar Protection Charm

The moon is often called upon by those in distress, and this traditional prayer from the Scottish Highlands and Islands is a good example of a prayer to ease a person in times of trouble. I have updated and adapted it for my use.

The New Moon

She of my love is the new moon
The of all creatures blessing her
Be mine a good purpose
Towards each creature of creation.
Holy be each thing
Which She illumines
Kindly be each deed
Which she reveals.
Be Her guidance on land
With all beset ones;
Be her guidance on the sea
With all distressed ones.
May the moon of moons
Be coming through thick clouds
On me and on every mortal
Who is coming through affliction.
May the moon my love
Be coming through the dense dark clouds
To me and to each one
Who is in tribulation.[28]

---

28. My adaptation based on "311 The New Moon" in Carmichael, *Carmina Gadelica*, 288.

Chapter 8
Wortcunning

The magical and healing knowledge of plants known as wortcunning is an essential skill in folk magic. In the modern world, this practice comes with all sorts of challenges. Not everyone is fortunate enough to have an outdoor space (myself included in days gone past)—in such cases, windowsills and doorsteps must suffice as places where the most essential of magical plants can be grown and nurtured. Space in friends' gardens and the ever-valuable community allotments are also invaluable as resources that enable us to hone our plant spirit skills and herbal knowledge. And when done knowledgeably and responsibly, foraging is also of course a great help. Nothing beats a witch's garden as a place of refuge and connection not only for the practitioner but also for all the wildlife and nature spirits in the surrounding area, as well as a place of great practical and magical resources.

I am blessed with a garden larger than my little cottage that has a diverse collection of plants and trees, but it did not appear instantly—it was something I've been honoured to grow and nurture over time. When I first came here originally, the garden was a large and neglected patch of lawn and little else. Instead of setting to work immediately to remodel and design the outdoor space, I instead listened to it, honouring the spirits I feel dwell there, seeking to build a cooperative relationship with them. In time, a garden has grown with them that thrives largely on its own and is a haven for all wild things.

When I sat with the space every day and listened to it, I tuned in to how different areas felt and noted how the sun moved around the area. Of the few plants that grew there, I sought to learn how they grew and where. I told the land that I loved it and would care for it, and I asked it to show me how I could help it grow. I left offerings of cream, water, and bird food for the land spirits and any passing wildlife. I visited a bramble patch at the back of the garden and told it that it could have a certain amount of space but no more than that—brambles are excellent for wildlife and frequently used in traditional fairy faith folk magic, but left unchecked in a domestic space, they grow unmanageable very quickly. In time I planted trees—heritage apple varieties, hawthorn, willow, and hazel all at the land spirits' request, trees that thrive in this area. Elder and holly self-seeded and were given permanent homes, as did a tiny yew tree that must have come from the yew tree in the village churchyard—he now resides in a large pot as an honoured resident. Yew takes many, many years to grow; it would not be suitable for him to be left to grow here. For the next few years, he will be an ally as a portal tree to the realms beyond, just as his parents are in the churchyard. I also grow spindle and witch hazel and am the caretaker to several baby oak trees that reside with me until I find them permanent homes where they can live out their millennia-long lives in peace.

Eventually I learnt the best place to clear a vegetable patch and herb garden, and I also created a sacred space in which I have a large fire bowl and several outdoor altars; these have grown since my first simple bowls of offerings placed upon the lawn but remain as places to honour the resident spirits and perform any healing or spell craft that can be done outside. The lawn has shrunk considerably; I now have large, sinewy flower beds where I grow a mixture of plants for magic, for healing, for their presence as plant spirits, or for their beauty. Everything is organically grown and allowed to self-seed and roam around the garden as it will year on year. If a plant thrives where it chooses and leaves where I planted it over a few seasons, that is fine—the plants know best. I also companion plant—that is, I let plants that naturally want to grow together do so, sometimes to protect one another from predators or disease, though I've noticed that some plants are just friends and like to be together. For example, my St. John's wort likes to grow near my lemon balm. While it stays where it was originally planted, it has also spread nearer and nearer the cottage every year until it popped up in a pot by my back door along with some self-seeded lemon balm, both of which now sit with pride of place on the back step as great allies for my protection, peace of mind, and inner calm. I also grow a lot of things in pots that may not suit the clayish West Country soil or they need lot of protection and attention to thrive in what is often a very wet and cool climate. My Irish Juniper is large and lush but needs to be drier than my garden is, so it sits in a large pot where it gets the air and winter sun and can dry out in between drenchings—a very Celtic plant, that, used to the high hills and mountains! Careful planting and positioning allows me to grow some plants from further afield, though most of my plant kin are native and a great many are wild that I cultivate and support. I welcome any plant that arrives unbidden or bring them home with great care from wild plant centres (so I don't damage the numbers of them in the wild).

When you choose the plants you want to grow, be aware first and foremost of what kinds of places they thrive in and aim to give them that. Let their natures dictate where they grow and you'll quickly find yourself thriving in relation with them. However, connecting with the land spirits residing in your own space is extremely important. If you have very little space amounting only to windowsills and doorsteps, these may be the same as your household spirits. And if you have a larger amount of outdoor space, they may be very different spirits.

Practicum
Connecting with the Spirits of the Garden

Perform this exercise at least once a month when beginning to build relationship with an outdoor space. Pay attention over the change of seasons, and make regular offerings to the land.

Begin by wandering the space, walking slowly and meditatively, seeking to be fully present and aware of all the small signals and information you can glean from a place. Choose a place to sit and a place to leave your offerings, ideally the same location each time, where you feel a greater sense of flow, power, or presence. Quite often, an area will point this place out via natural features: the base of a tree that seems ideally shaped or positioned, a natural area of light or shade, or a liminal area—the edge or gateway zone—but every place is different. The first challenge is to try to feel that out.

When you have found the right place, sit down and breathe with the land; if there are trees and plants growing around you be aware of their roots and breathe down into the earth, breathing up into the trunks and branches, stems and leaves. Just be with this a while…nature, especially plants can be slow so slowing down and being present to them helps to align us with their rhythms. After a while, ask that a guardian of the earth here come forth to meet you and advise you in the care of this patch of land. Be gentle and patient…take plenty of time concentrating on being present with the earth, not separate from it. Notice any little shifts in consciousness you may experience as most often this is the way such spirits will make their presence felt. Don't expect something visual or being communicated with in words although this may happen. Look instead for shifts in how something feels, what calls your attention, what fresh thoughts and perceptions you may have. You may feel a presence as if someone is standing before you. Let yourself be immersed in the experience, and fine-tune what you perceive. Allow time to receive any communication directed to you. Ask perhaps for a sense of the history of the land and what it needs to thrive. Perhaps ask what one thing you can do straight away to begin to honour this or what offerings it likes to accept.

Repeat this tuning in often—train yourself as time goes on to become sensitive to the nuances and subtle expressions of the land and its guardian spirit. Eventually, you'll notice your sense of the area expand and weave in many other spirits who are present. Learn to read the land's expression in the play of the wind in the trees, the flight of the birds, where butterflies soak up the sunlight, when the sparrows tap on the window.

The Apple Tree Man

The apple holds a special place in Celtic and British folklore, and the importance of orchards as places of nature's abundance and spirits is found across the British Isles. There's something liminal and magical about orchards, placed as they are in between wild and domestic spaces. Full of wildlife and reflecting each season, apple trees seem to age rapidly becoming gnarly and rugged looking whilst still quite young but may live for many years. The oldest tree in the orchard is considered the home of the apple tree man who oversees the orchard and tends to the land's fertility. He appears in folk tales as a kindly but strange old man offering warnings or advice. The British otherworld or realm of the spirits is known in medieval literature as Avalon, (drawn from earlier Celtic lore, meaning "the Isle of Apples") and is considered to have one of its physical entrances at Glastonbury in Somerset and its surrounding Avalon Marshes where I live that surround Glastonbury with water every season. In times past, this flooding made it an island in the truest sense. Avalon is also associated with its lord, Avalloch, the father of Morgan le Fay of Arthurian myth, who is also named after the apple, from the Brythonic *abal* and the Romano-British *Aballava*—"place of the apple trees," a possible hint at the survival of this tradition into the local folklore. To me, Avalloch certainly is the apple tree man, spirit keeper of the orchards, and the guardian of souls in Avalon's care.

If you have an outdoor space fortunate enough to contain some trees, take time to tune in to them and the plants. See if one of the trees is a lead tree spirit or elder of the garden like the apple tree man. The tree needn't be apple, although that has a lot of folklore attached—it can be any tree. This spirit should be key in building relationship with your patch of land and the spirits within it as well as the key to bringing blessings to the whole area.

Practicum
Vision Journey to Connect with Plant Spirits

After you've found a plant to work with magically or grow in your garden, take time to befriend its spirit and learn from it just as you would from any book or website about its qualities and virtues.

Just as you did when contacting the guardian of the land, sit with the plant and breathe slowly, aiming to breathe with it, roots to leaves. Slow down and seek alignment and unity with the plant in your awareness. Close your eyes and see it in your inner vision: how does it look and feel to you now? Touch it and smell it. Ask to meet its indwelling spirit, looking out for changes in consciousness, subtle shifts of feeling, and new thoughts. You may get an inner sense of it as a being with a clear form, but be aware that it is a shifting thing—its true being may be more subtle.

Ask the spirit about itself and direct your care towards it. Show that you appreciate its being, its unique beauty. What communication do you feel in return? Take time and ask what the plant needs to thrive, how you can support it, as well as the ideal times to gather a little of it for your use. Does it have a preferred way of working magic with you? A preferred showing of gratitude afterwards? Nothing is better at plant magic than the plant spirits themselves. See this as an unfolding relationship that builds connection so that you can learn directly from the plants. Try to set aside linear human thinking and enter into an organic magical connection based on cocreation with the spirits.

Plants for the Witch's Garden

If you have the space, growing your own plants and herbs for magic and healing is a very empowering thing that will help your relationship with the spirits immeasurably. In addition, space to dry and prepare your herbs can be found easier than you think if you hang things from windows or make a rack over the hearth.

Because every garden or growing space is different, it's important to pay attention to conditions when growing plants—not everything you want to grow may thrive in your space. However, if you befriend plant spirits and attend to them as spirit kin, you'll find that you can grow far more than you ever realised.

The list here is not exhaustive or complete; the topic of magical herbs could fill a book on its own, and there are many out there to assist you. What follows is a small selection of the ones I've found most useful for getting started.

> *Basil (Ocimum basilicum):* Basil is useful for money magic and luck, as well as for cooking. Basil is also good for purification and clearing the mind and spirit. A potted basil will need to be kept in a warm and sunny place and spend its winters inside. Anoint prosperity sigils or candles with basil oil, either as an essential oil or basil-infused olive oil.
>
> *Bay (Laurus nobilis):* Grown as a small tree or shrub, bay is excellent for money spells and in incense to attract prosperity and success. Also

good in cooking. Growing bay by the front door attracts money into the house.

Bee balm (Monarda didyma): Bee balm is a good spirit who brings enthusiasm and makes an excellent offering to spirits. Bee balm is useful as an anti-inflammatory herb for coughs and fever. It can be a little aggressive, so plant it in a good position for it to spread. This plant prefers sun and grows well in beds and flower borders.

Calendula (Calendula officinalis): Calendula is excellent as a skin healer and soother, and it's also useful in healing spells and to soothe discord. It makes distressed people feel supported and is good in solar magic. Best sown annually, it can grow in pots or beds under full sun.

Catnip (Nepeta cataria): Beloved by cats, catnip is also useful in beauty, love, and happiness spells. Catnip attracts good luck and friendly spirits. Add catnip to simmer pots for peace and a happy home. Catnip likes to grow under the full sun in beds or containers.

Chamomile (Matricaria chamomilla): Chamomile is excellent for easing stress, for dream spells, and in charms of protection and reassurance. It can be added to the bath or made into a tea to ease distress, and chamomile tea is wonderful for children whether by itself, served with mint, or mixed with honey in warm milk. Chamomile is easy to grow and very hardy. It likes sunny spots and free-draining soil but otherwise can be left alone to do its thing, blessing the garden with its scent.

Echinacea (Echinacea purpurea): Echinacea is an excellent herb to use in healing and health spells. When its root is taken as a tisane, it helps with all illnesses and strengthens the immune system. This is a hardy perennial that adapts well to many climates, preferring full sun to partial shade.

Elecampane (Inula helenium): Elecampane is a powerful spirit ally whose other name is "elfwort." A protector against bad spirits that also attracts good ones, it is a wonderful ally in the garden and can be grown as an offering to the spirits. Dried elecampane root is powerful against coughs and chest infections and can help ease the symptoms of asthma. Its strong, perfumy scent dispels all stuck energy or sadness from a space and fills it with blessings. The fumes of elecampane alone in a simmer pot have been known to ease coughs and tight chests. Elecampane grows to 1.5 to 2 metres tall, so it should be positioned wisely. It likes full sun to partial shade as well as moist, well-drained soil. Because it is a perennial, a patch of it will expand year after year, flowering after its second year and thereafter.

Horehound (Marrubium vulgare): Horehound is useful for protection, visions, creativity, and inspiration. Medicinally, it is excellent to ease coughs. Horehound grows best in beds and can tolerate partial shade.

Hyssop (Hyssopus officinalis): I love hyssop and find it to be a very beautiful addition to my garden, as well as magically powerful. Hyssop can be used for purification, protection, and healing magic, and I find it especially useful for boundaries and to protect women. Hyssop can be used in teas to ease sore throats and coughs.

Lavender (Lavandula angustifolia): Every garden should have lavender—soothing, calming, and healing, it helps the heart ease of sorrow and is highly versatile in herbal medicine incense blends and even cooking. Lavender is excellent for love, healing, and purification spells as well as fairy contact. Burn lavender as incense to attract peace and calm. Lavender grows best in full sun in either a container or a garden bed.

Lemon balm (Melissa officinalis): Lemon balm is beloved by bees and is so easy to grow it should have a place in every witch's garden. A plant sacred to Artemis, lemon balm eases the spirit, is calming and soothing and can bring light back where someone is experiencing sorrow. Lemon balm does well in sun or partial shade, in containers or in a bed. It grows rapidly and can become invasive so may be best in wilder areas of the garden or grown in a pot.

Mint (Mentha spicata): Mint is good for prosperity spells, love and health magic, and protection. Peppermint oil is an excellent energetic cleanser if waved across someone's energy field. Mint calls upon good spirits and has a freshening energy that dispels gloomy spirits and difficult emotions from the atmosphere. Mint is excellent as a refreshing tea or for easing stomach problems and is often a favourite with children who tend to like the taste even when unwell. Because it grows very fast, it's best suited for containers.

Mugwort (Artemisia vulgaris): Mugwort is excellent for divination and purification. It assists in increasing psychic abilities and works well in dream magic. Roman soldiers carried it to ensure safe travel, and placed in your shoe, it will ease fatigue. It can be drunk as a tisane to assist in spirit journeys and added to an incense. Mugwort tisane can be used to cleanse your magical and ritual tools. Mugwort likes partial sun and works well in pots. Caution: Mugwort is helpful for menstrual issues under herbalist supervision but is dangerous for pregnant women and those who bleed heavily. If these are issues even potential for you, handle with care and seek the advice of a medical herbalist.

Illustration 8: Mugwort

Mullein (Verbascum thapsus): Mullein is excellent for cough and flu as well as for making hag torches. A powerful and friendly spirit presence in the garden, mullein is also beloved of fairies. It is easy to grow and likes partial sun and shade but will self-seed prolifically once established.

Rose (Rosa x damascena): Rose is wonderful for love and healing spells where it soothes the heart. It also is beloved by the spirits and is excellent as an offering. Roses can be tricky to grow, but perhaps the most important detail is to make sure they have rich soil and are fed yearly. Different types of rose need different conditions, and some can grow in pots for individual care, making them suitable in smaller spaces. As a rule, they need sunny spots and rich, well-drained soil.

Rosemary (Salvia rosmarinus): Rosemary is a must in a witch's garden. A highly protective plant, it can be hung over boundaries or tied with red thread to draw luck and love. Rosemary is excellent when burnt for protection as is its essential oil. Dried rosemary can also be added to incense or burnt in herb bundles. Rosemary works well with other strong aromatic herbs in simmer pots to clear and refresh a space or offer stimulation to someone who is in need of rest but must endure. Rosemary tisane hair rinses are excellent for dandruff and to make the hair lush and shiny, brown hair in particular. For success, carry rosemary in your pocket when doing tests or exams. Rosemary is an evergreen shrub that can grow quite large, requiring full sun and drier earth. It can also be quite happy in a pot.

Sage (Salvia officinalis): Although many think of white sage (*Salvia apiana*) when it comes to magic, it has a host of ethical issues and is not part of the European tradition. Common garden sage is also a powerful magical herb for purification and protection. It is useful for spells invoking wisdom and unseen solutions to a problem. Sage tea works well to heal and relieve cold and flu, and it will force through a fever if a lingering virus needs burning out, though only use it with healthy adults—it is a strong remedy! The sage spirit is good to work with, a powerful and warming ally. Garden sage is also wonderful in homemade herbal bundles for burning and can be used in prosperity spells and charm bags. Sage likes drier ground in full sun and can be grown in beds and containers.

Soapwort (Saponaria officinalis): Soapwort is a very pretty and easy to grow little herb with pale pink flowers that thrives in garden flower borders and beds and spreads easily. This herb should not be taken internally. When added to warm water, crushed fresh or dried soapwort creates a soft, gentle lather. It is excellent as a natural soap and can be used for everything for which you would use a detergent. However, the added benefit of using soapwort is that it can be used with other herbs and natural ingredients, allowing you to invoke its spirit along with other plant spirits to make cleansing work all the more magically effective. This plant is good for cleansing ritual items and clothing as well as boundaries, doors, and windows. It is also safe on skin and hair for ritual bathing, as well as for healing bruising.

St. John's wort (Hypericum perforatum): St. John's wort is an excellent protective herb and good for herbal medicine to ease depression. When infused in oil, it can ease aches and pains and heal wounds. It adds great power to any spell and is easy to grow. It likes full sun but is tough and adaptable, taking well to both beds and containers.

Sweet woodruff (Galium odoratum): Sweet woodruff smells wonderful and is excellent in incense and potpourri. This herb can be added as a flavouring to the Mai bowl, a wine mixture made in celebration of Mayday or Bealtaine. Called "the Master of the Woods," it works well in summer-themed magic—love and prosperity spells. Its spirit is friendly, and it is a beautiful perennial plant to grow, appearing in early spring in shady areas.

Thyme (Thymus vulgaris): An herb related to bravery, thyme is also excellent for relieving colds, chest infections, and asthma—and in cooking, of course. Thyme likes to grow in sun or partial shade either in a bed or containers.

Valerian (Valeriana officinalis): Valerian is an excellent herb for the nervous system. Relaxing and restorative, it is helpful for shock, panic, and anxiety as well as insomnia and nervous exhaustion. It's a good herb to have around for emergencies. Magically, valerian can be used for protection and counter-magic. It is said to protect against lightning and the evil eye.

Vervain (Verbena officinalis): Vervain is a powerful herb for general purification as well as for consecrating magical tools. It is excellent to drink as a protective herb before spirit work and eases anxiety. Vervain likes sun or shade and will self-seed prolifically once established.

Yarrow (Achillea millefolium): Yarrow is helpful for all sorts of magic—love, divination, protection, and courage spells, and it can bring allies and friendship to you. Yarrow tincture is excellent as an insect repellent and can soothe and shrink insect bites, especially mosquitoes and midges. Applied to scratches and minor wounds, yarrow is powerfully styptic, stopping bleeding. Hang yarrow by your bed for magical dreams and to learn about spirits. A tough and hardy plant, yarrow grows best in beds and full sun.

Magical Woods for Wands, Sticks, and Staffs

In addition to plants, many outdoor spaces have trees that together form a vital part of our magical work as allies and practical tools. All trees have different virtues and energies, and many species have long histories of use both magical and practical. What follows is a selection of the most widely used, but you are encouraged to use what feels right to you. Always keep practicality, sustainability, and ecological responsibility in mind in your work.

Alder (Alnus glutinosa): Alder has good oracular and protective virtues and is good for helping instill confidence, learning to handle emotions, and calm upset. The wood was a favourite for shields, and carrying alder can help shield you from hurtful comments and unkind eyes.

Apple (Malus x domestica): Apple is a tree of the otherworld in both British and Irish tradition, where Avalon, or *Emain Ablach*, meaning "the Isle of Apples," is a place of goodness and healing where a traveller may find ease and comfort. Apple is good for healing and soothing the spirit as well as for sacred sexuality. A tree of wholeness, it was once sacred and is a very important tree in the West Country, where ancient apple orchards abound. The apple tree man or apple spirit is a well-known god local to Somerset, where I live, who resides in the oldest tree in the orchard and is responsible for the whole orchard's bounty. The old tradition of wassailing is to honour and seek his blessing for the coming year by offering him gifts of warm cider and hanging toast in the branches as offerings.

Ash (Fraxinus excelsior): The ash is considered to be a tree of the air spirits and is good for workings do with healing, and regeneration. Ash is a strong wood, which was favoured for spears in the Celtic period. Like the yew and the oak, ash was considered sacred in Ireland, and the Bilé Tortan was considered one of the main five sacred trees, known as Bilé, in all of Ireland, where, like the Norse Yggdrasil it functioned as a world tree, connecting all the realms and the six directions. For these reasons ash has often been the chosen wood for a staff by conjurers, cunning folk, and pellars (hex breakers—from the word "expel").

Birch (Betula pendula): Birch is protective, and bundles of birch twigs can be used to "beat the bounds" of your home to drive away evil influences as well as to lightly beat against the skin to clear away stuck energies or spirit intrusions. Birch has a strong inner light that repels and is feared by bad spirits.

Blackthorn (Prunus spinosa): Blackthorn has strong associations with the otherworld and fairy folk and is often favoured by West Country cunning folk as powerfully protective and repellent against ill will. It is also the chosen wood to make blasting rods for maleficium or magical attacks, sometimes as the best defence. A classic example of a blasting rod is found in the Museum of Witchcraft and Magic in Boscastle, Cornwall, where three blackthorn twigs are twisted together and tied with black and red thread, their many long thorns still attached.[29] Although I have seen blasting rods of all sorts of designs including finely turned and polished examples, I've found that the less work done on the wood, the more powerful they are. Thorns from these trees can also be useful in certain healing spells where they may work like a magical version of acupuncture needles.

---

29. "Rod," Museum of Witchcraft and Magic, accessed February 27, 2024 https://museumofwitchcraftandmagic.co.uk/object/wand-rod/.

Elder (Sambucus nigra): Elder is a tree of the fairies and home to the Elder Mother, or Lady Elder as she is known in Cornwall, where elder leaves are hung in stables for the protection of horses from flies and other insects. However, elder must never be cut without the Elder Mother's permission and should never be burnt, lest it invite the ill will of the spirit world. One story local to Somerset, "The Elder Witch," tells of a witch who can shapeshift into an elder tree and suffers harm in her human body when the tree is cut. The elder is one of the most useful trees in the British woodland for healing and herbal remedies; every part of it has medicinal or practical value. The flowers are good against fevers and can be used to make elderflower syrup, a delicious drink that makes an excellent spirit offering. The berries are highly nutritious and have strong antiviral and antioxidant properties, and they can be served as tea or made into a syrup that soothes coughs, colds, and all lung infections. Both leaves and flowers are detoxifying and diuretic, and the bark was once used as a purgative, though this is not advised. The leaves on their own make an excellent bug repellent and, whilst weak and hollow, elder wood can make powerful magical tools when turned into whistles or flutes for calling spirits.

Gorse (Ulex europaeus): Yellow gorse is a fiery plant considered excellent for fire magic and purification as well as for love spells, where it adds to the rising of passion and desire. Gorse and furze have long been considered highly protective against fairy attack and abduction, and in one historical case in Wales recounts where a person long beset by fairies slept in a circle of gorse for protection.[30] All yellow flowers and especially gorse are placed on the doorsteps of Irish homes to this day at the special time of Bealtaine/May Day to protect against fairy influence.

Hawthorn (Crataegus monogyna): This tree belongs to the fairies and should never be burnt. Old hawthorns—especially those standing alone—should never be cut down lest they incur the fairies' wrath.

---

30. Wirt Sikes, *British Goblins: Welsh Folk-Lore, Fairy Mythology, Legends and Traditions* (EP Publishing, 1973), 115. Originally published 1880, Sampson and Low.

This tradition is particularly strong in Ireland but can be found all over the British Isles. In the West Country, where I live, practitioners often called upon the assistance and protection of the fairies by performing their magic beneath the branches of a hawthorn, offering the spirits gifts of food and drink in friendship and exchange, a practice that undoubtedly goes back very far indeed and is specifically a Celtic and British thing rather than from the medieval European magic found in much of witchcraft practice. The hawthorn is associated with the coming of summer; Bealtaine, Calan Mai, and May Day celebrations are often focused on the coming of the hawthorn blossom, which is strongly associated with fertility and sexuality, though it is taboo to bring it inside the home lest it offend the fairies. As green kin, hawthorn is a great heart healer that aids in circulation as well as in soothing feelings of heartbreak and depression. However, its fairy associations make it a poor choice of walking stick—West Country tradition suggests it brings bad luck to journeys and leads people astray.

Hazel (Corylus avellana): Known as the diviner, hazel is useful for rites of divination, seeking wisdom, and increasing communication. Dried hazel leaves are a good addition to incense for all themes Mercury- and communication-related as well as for finding lost objects or hidden knowledge. It is also an excellent ally for increasing creativity.

Juniper (Juniperus communis): Juniper is a powerful tree in Scottish Gaelic tradition, though it can be found as a tree and shrub all across the British Isles and in Ireland. In Scotland, it is used for saining; burnt juniper creates a sacred cleansing smoke that was used to ritually bless spaces and remove illness and baneful influences, and it was also considered to be highly protective from evil and ill wishes in Ireland and the rest of Britain, where it was used in a myriad of ways magically and medicinally.

Oak (Quercus spp.): Oak is the wood of doorways—it is considered a good and holy tree, the chosen wood of church doorways and castles. It is strongly protective but also allows an opening of the ways for spirit flight; oak's name in the Ogham alphabet—*duir* or *dara* as it is known in Irish—has the same root as the word "druid";

in other words, "one who has the wisdom of the oak." *Draoi* (pronounced "dree") is the Irish word for a magical practitioner, though it sometimes can refer to a druid or even a magician or diviner. Often overlooked in British magic, listening to the wind in oak leaves is a natural form of divination, and old oaks are always homes for the spirits who flock to them in vast numbers, using them both as residences and a way between this world and the other.

Rowan (Sorbus aucuparia): One of my very favourite magical trees, rowan is a strong ally and is also known as the "quicken tree" because it is usually one of the first to take root in new ground and it quickens and lends fertility and initiating energy to any spell or working to really get things going when change is needed. Rowan is the best of the protective trees but it also helps the practitioner see where the issue or problem lies. Rowan twigs tied with red thread is a traditional protection charm found all across Ireland and the British Isles, placed above doors and windows and around babies' cribs to protect from ill intent, magic, malicious spirits, and fairy attack. It is still used in some farms and homes from Scotland to the West Country today where there is an old saying:

> *Rowan-tree and red thread*
> *Put the witches to their speed*[31]

A necklace or bracelet or rowan berries can be worn and was a popular protection charm in Cornwall. Sometimes the crossbeam of a fireplace is made of rowan wood to protect the home and bar the entry of any spirits down the chimney.

Scots Pine (Pinus sylvestris): Associated energetically with fire and air, this tree is helpful for gaining of wisdom and clear thinking. In this way, its virtues are excellent for protective and cleansing magic, particularly against ill wishes that cause confusion and a loss of direc-

---

31. Robert Chambers, *Popular Rhymes of Scotland* (W & R Chambers, 1870), 328. For more on the rowan and the magical qualities of trees, see my book *Celtic Tree Magic* (Llewellyn Publications, 2014).

tion. Pine is also good for healing and filling a space with positive energies and good spirits.

Willow (Salix alba): Willow has watery energy, and its virtues are all connected to flow and the lunar, intuitive, and emotional sides of life. Good for dreamwork, healing, and moon mysteries, especially menstrual and birthing magic. Willow bark is excellent for easing pain and reducing fevers due to its high salicylic acid content, the key ingredient in aspirin.

Yew (Taxus baccata): Yew trees are usually associated with life after death and the spirit realms. Some of the oldest trees in Britain and Ireland are yews, and they can live for thousands of years in constant regeneration. In Britain these ancient yews are often found in churchyards, and some scholars believe that ancient yews in churchyards mark where earlier pre-Christian temples must have stood—after all, they usually predate their accompanying churches—but little archaeological evidence exists to verify, as few digs are done underneath churches. Yew is the final tree in the Irish ogham alphabet where it stands for the world tree or the otherworld. Ireland once had numerous sacred trees called the *Bilé* where kings were coronated and large gatherings of religious and legal importance were held in the pre-Christian era. Of these were five especially sacred Bilé, two of which—the Eó Rossa and the Eó Mugna—were yew trees, pointing to their importance. Because the yew is related to fate, death, and otherworld spirit connection, it is excellent for workings with spirits. However, caution must be taken: All parts of this plant are highly toxic. Welsh longbows used to be made of yew wood, and it makes an excellent handle for magical knives. Touching the wood seems to have no ill effects; however, breathing in its smoke or eating its berries are not advised.

Practicum
A Charm for Gathering Herbs with Magical Purposes

When gathering herbs for magic, I like to be as conscious of the plant spirit as possible, always seeking to use the herb with its permission and thanking it for its assistance. I therefore pick with great care, taking only what I need and being sure to do as little harm as possible to the plant and its surrounding area.

I also say this charm to honour the spirit of the plant, calling upon the Irish goddess Airmed, of herbs and healing. I work frequently with Airmed when gardening or preparing herbs for use and feel my practice has deepened as a result. What follows isn't from traditional English witchcraft but is part of my personal practice. You are welcome to follow it or adapt its words to suit your own herbal magics.

Hail to thee, holy herb
Growing in the ground
All things were blessed
When you were found
You are good for many needs
And heal many a wound
In the name of Airmed,
I take thee from the ground![32]

Working with Plant Spirits

Plant spirit medicine is something found the world over, essentially boiling down to the simple art of making medicinal herbal remedies and spirit-based potions with the plant spirits' assistance and empowerment. The theosophy movement of nineteenth- and early twentieth-century England and America promoted the idea that plant spirits were intelligent beings called "devas" (a Hindu term) who could aid in human development. The term is still used today in Western magical traditions, but plant spirits have long been present in spiritual and magical traditions to connect and work with in various ways. At around the same time as the theosophists, Edward Bach produced his famous flower remedies that use the essence of the plant spirit for human healing and spiritual assistance, another practice that also has echoes in older practices. In Old Celtic and British magical traditions, much is made of the

---

32. Hewett, *Nummits and Crummits*, 81. The original calls on Jesus but has been adapted for my own purposes to reflect my own work and Irish heritage, calling instead upon the Irish goddess of herbal knowledge.

dew gathered at dawn at certain times of year—especially at Bealtaine (May 1) when the life force of the earth is high—similar to how flower remedies are produced, placing blooms in fresh spring water in sunlight. Another method for making flower essences is to boil the plant matter in spring water rather like a traditional potion or to leave the plant and water to energise and create the essence together under moon or starlight in certain places or under certain weather conditions. All these techniques use the great magical adaptability of fresh, living spring water and the plant spirits to create the potion, essence, remedy, or brew. The spirits of fresh spring water can also work with the powers of place to make vibrational remedies from healing sacred sites for example.

Practicum
To Make a Flower Essence

First, spend time with the plant to connect with its spirit. Through this connection, you will learn how to work with it as well as what an essence made with it can be used for. There are lots of books on this practice that often (but not always) tell of a flower essence that bears some relation to its uses as an herbal remedy, but nothing is as good or as powerful as building your relationship with a plant spirit first. Without this connection, we are merely going through the motions and the essence will not be effective. Equally a clear understanding of this reveals to us what flower or plant essences we should make and why.

When making a flower essence, you may find the plant wants you to make it in a different way, in which case you should follow its guidance. Generally speaking, the following two procedures work best with most plants.

The Sun Method

As close to the dawn as possible, select a clear, dry day to gather a fresh bloom of the plant or the best and most perfect-looking leaves if it isn't flowering. Place what you collect in a clear glass bowl of fresh spring water. It's best if the sun is rising as you do so. Ask the spring water and the plant to work with the sun to make a healing essence, sending it your gratitude. Then place the bowl on the earth next to the plant under direct sunlight. Leave it all day or until small bubbles can be seen in the water, which is when the essence has potentised. When it is time, drain the water without the bloom into a dark glass bottle to the halfway point, and top up the remaining half of the bottle with brandy or another strong alcoholic spirit to preserve it. The result is known as the mother tincture and is very powerful.

The Boiling Method

This method is also best with fresh spring water. In a pan (ideally glass or copper), boil the water for around ten minutes. If you can, use a real fire or at least a flame from a gas cooker to add additional fire energy. As you can imagine, some plants respond better with this boiling, fiery method than others. Each essence should be made on a case-by-case basis in close connection with the plant spirit for guidance. Wait for the water to cool completely. When it has, drain it without the bloom into a dark glass bottle to the halfway point, and top up the remaining half of the bottle with brandy or another strong alcoholic spirit to preserve it.

Preparing and Using an Essence

To make an essence for use, take another small dark glass bottle and place in it three drops of the mother tincture and top with brandy. This creates the essence for use in much the same way as the Bach flower remedies in the shops.

These essences are most often taken in water, a couple of drops in a large glass of water drank several times a day. You can also use an essence in bathwater, when watering plants, or in cleaning mixes and potions for use around the home. The possibilities are endless.

Spring Water Versus Tap Water

The reason we use fresh spring water is because it can be understood as having a living spirit within it compared to tap water, which is often understood as energetically deadened due to all the processing and filtration it goes through. I personally am blessed to live near several springs that have healthy drinkable water, a rare privilege these days. Many practitioners have to make compromises. Spring water bought from the shop is better than tap water, and tap water will do in a pinch—just add some life energy to it by blessing it and stirring it in a clockwise, charging, empowering direction.

Be aware that although not all spring or river water is safe to drink, that may not mean you can't use it all—it may be that your local spring water is ideal for magic just not for human drinking. Use common sense always.

Magical Waters

Water is an immensely powerful magical tool that can be used as is or after asking the spirits within it to assist us with our intentions. The Celts of the distant past honoured water and water sources as places of the spirits—rivers were the embodiments of river goddesses, and wells and springs were meeting places with the other world. Rain and storms were also the product of the gods, especially Taranis the storm god, who brought change. There's also a belief that water gathered at certain times and certain places contains unique energies, a belief we can use to finesse and empower our spells and potions. Often the best water to use and what makes it so is deeply intuitive, but here is a broad guide.

While they aren't commonly found in every garden, many old homes have wells, springs, and streams passing through their land and are included here because water is such an important part of our magic inside and outside the home.

Spring water: Earth and water energy combined, water goddesses, raising energy, adding life force, good for charging with specific intentions

Moon water: Purifying, cleansing, increasing intuition, relating and connecting, dreamwork, web-mending, and travelling

Sun water: Healing, empowering, strengthening, positivity, confidence building

Stream water: Gentle, purifying, cleansing

Lake water: To bring peace, reflection, rest, and contemplation; aids in problem-solving

Pond water: Relaxation and self-reflection, can be used for binding

Rain water: Change, growth, protection, cleansing, releasing

River water: Creating changes, warding, neutralising harm and ill will, curse lifting, moving forwards, sudden insights

Snow water: Purity, a fresh start, transformation

Ice/Frost water: Purity, transforming, bringing change, releasing grief and stuckness

Storm water: Strength, power, force, release

Marsh water: Otherworld and spirit contact, ancestor connection, divination

Waterfall water: Power, success

Well water: Healing, spirit connection, blessing

Dew water: Fairy, plant spirits, love, beauty

Mist water: Spirit invocation, liminality, calling in the otherworld, fairies, ancestors, the dead

Harbour/Port water: Safety, protection, abundance, support

Sea water: Healing, cleansing, banishing, protecting, neutralising, spirit contact

Water from where rivers meet or estuaries: Liminality, connecting, bringing change, adding large amounts of power

Waters of saints and gods: Many springs and wells are dedicated to a specific god or saint, as are some rivers and lakes. Each of these bodies of water will also resonate with these particular beings, and the water from these places can be used to call upon or invoke these beings and their virtues and areas of assistance. For example, a well or spring dedicated to Brigit—saint or goddess—will be especially powerful when working with fire, creativity, healing, the protection of women and children, and so on.

Practicum
Ice and Snow Spell for Transformation

This spell is obviously weather dependent—although I know some would use frozen water from the freezer, it just isn't the same—it's not the temperature of the water but its energetic pattern and the state of its indwelling spirit that is key. You can use this technique to unfreeze a stuck situation or to find a sense of release and change when you are holding on to feelings of circumstances that hold you back.

Gather some snow in a glass container. As you do so, give thanks to the water spirits within it and the spirits of the land and sky where you are. Take the snow to the place where you wish to perform your magic. As before, ritually cleanse yourself and invoke its indwelling spirit by chanting or repeating something suitable in your own words. Here's one example:

Spirit of the snow, I call to you now!
Spirit of the snow, I call to you now!
Attend to me in kinship!

When you feel you have built up some power and feel or sense the spirit of the snow being present and attentive to you, discuss your situation with it as you might a friend. You may get into a dialogue where advice is given, or you could receive images or symbols. After a while, place your hands upon the snow and send your feelings about the situation into it or write your feelings down on a piece of paper and ask for a solution or a breakthrough to occur. This is important and will look different for everyone, but it is essential that you ask for a transformation of your situation, a breakthrough. If you have a sense of how you want this to occur, you may ask for this specifically but be aware experiencing stuckness in a situation may mean that you are resisting changing your direction to a more fulfilling one. If that's the case, ask for your ideas and attitudes to be transformed to something more effective.

Really take your time and place your effort into placing your feelings and communication into the snow, continuing until you feel yourself giving some of your energy to it. Then close and complete your spell by thanking the snow spirit and placing your written feelings into it together with any objects you associate with the situation (for example, a house key for a new house if that's what you desire). Finally, place a tight lid onto the container and leave it on your altar or another safe, suitable place to let the snow melt at its own pace. When it has completely turned to water, leave it for another day or two, and then return the water to the earth, taking the stuck energy or circumstances with it. Afterwards, wash the container out with salted water.

Chapter 9
Familiars and Other Spirits

Wise women and cunning folk may have many spirit helpers and allies, beings of elemental presence, the spirits of lakes and holy wells, or spirts of the land, air, or fire, but of course those allies may include spirits of the home and hearth, spirits of the ancestors and the fairy folk, and animal spirits—familiars.

Familiars may take several forms and were traditionally considered to be tightly bound to a magical worker to do their bidding and represent them and their interests out in the world, allowing remote viewing of situations, people, and places when in the worker's stead. Familiars can be created by will and powerful magic into thought-forms given life and anchored to a particular host object, or they can also be spirits in animal form that choose to work with a person. They can also be physical animals that have a strong psychic bond with their owner.

Cunning folk and wise women would often have one or several living animal familiars who would be bound to perform their will and on occasion be ridden by the practitioner's spirit in spirit flight. Tales of wounding a white hare and finding the next day that the old woman in the village was limping due to a wound in the same place illustrate this and the strength of the bond between witch and familiar. The two are effectively one being when engaged in magical workings, separating again after completion and uniting again the next time. The most common animals in these tales are hares or rabbits, cats, dogs, birds, and of course toads, a popular and evocative option. Historically are also reports of less conventional animals such as flies or bees. Working with these animal spirits either alive or in spirit form is a gift that comes easily to some and less so to others but is generally beneficial and universally recommended as an important part of the wild witch's skills—connecting with a familiar is invaluable to assist the worker in connecting with whole new vistas of practice and possibility.

Living familiars are usually with the practitioner from birth or come to them of their own volition from the wild to live with them, whereupon they spend most of their lives in close companionship with the wise woman who is rarely seen without them. Historically we know from the Scottish witch trials that it was common for a witch to suckle their familiars on their own blood as part of the magical bonding they underwent together.[33] Other practitioners, especially today, will still give their animal familiar a few drops of their blood in their food from time to time for the same reasons so that the animal is "blood of my blood"—they are bound as kin.[34]

Living in close proximity, a familiar will sleep with and be the practitioner's near-constant companion to be treated with great affection. When the time is deemed right, the practitioner will begin to work with the familiar and explore what they can do together, and the most common practice is spirit flight.

After preparations have been made, the animal sits before the practitioner, who rests their hands on either side of the animal's head and looks deep into their eyes, murmuring a charm until a light trance is achieved. Such charms vary from person to person, but it is generally useful to name the animal and your intent: for example, "[Name of familiar], come spirit walk with me this night." The phrase is repeated over and over until the animal and the spirit walker are in trance-like unison. This may take practice, and it will certainly take patience! The practitioner will then journey into the spirit world with the familiar or in the spirit version of their shared surroundings to glean any local knowledge they may require. Alternatively and more

---

33. Emma Wilby, *Cunning Folk and Familiar Spirits: Shamanistic Visionary Traditions in Early Modern British Witchcraft and Magic* (Sussex Academic Press, 2013), 170.

34. This is obviously not something to take lightly. It can be very dangerous for the practitioner and the animal, so I do not advise it. For those who pursue this practice, great care and all sensible precautions must be taken.

advanced is sending the familiar off to do the practitioner's will, in which case it physically departs and carries out the practitioner's bidding, during which the familiar's eyes serve as the practitioner's as they are joined in spirit flight and vision.

There are a great many advantages to having a physical animal familiar; when not working consciously with you, they can still be of support and protection. While it depends greatly on an individual animal's species and temperament, it is generally thought that cat familiars are excellent walkers between the worlds and are first rate at seeing spirits and alerting you to their presence. Birds are similar and can serve as excellent guards and alarm bells—ravens, crows, and owls are particularly good at working in dreams and bringing messages from the spirit world, the gods, and the dead. Dogs are fantastic allies for protection and seeing spirits particularly with ancestor work; their presence has a great natural effect on negative or stuck energy—many lingering ill-wishing spirits will simply flee an area when a dog is set loose within it. And if a dog ever looks intimidated or frightened, take heed because something threatening is around! Toads are traditionally considered a great aid to magical workers both alive and in spirit form; in fact, tradition says that letting a toad be the first to enter a new home is guaranteed to draw blessings to the place.[35]

The limitations to working with living animal familiars are that they are mostly used for remote viewing that supports your work and seeing the unseen around you. A spirit familiar is more flexible in that it can do its own magic and act on your instructions in a more independent way—spirits of animal form that accept working with you can be very powerful and helpful indeed and support your work but also your inner development and evolution by helping you draw out their qualities within you.

Familiars may also be made as thought-forms to perform specific tasks, sometimes for set periods of time. This magic is quite straightforward but needs careful consideration and responsible handling. A thought-form that is weak or ill-formed will be ineffective, just as a thought-form that is too powerful or badly and inaccurately focused can wreak havoc, especially if not effectively dismantled or its creator dies.

---

35. Gemma Garry, *The Black Toad: West Country Witchcraft and Magic* (Troy Books, 2011), 73.

We will look at attaining both types of familiars, but let's first look at creating a thought-form.

Thought-Form Creation

Before anything else, be very clear what you want your familiar to do and what kind of form would be most suitable. Thought-forms are often modelled after the elements of earth, air, or water, but this doesn't have to be so. And though I would advise against using fire for a thought-form (fire beings can be more dangerous and unpredictable than other forms), whatever you create can be unique—draw it or make it out of clay if you wish to give it shape. As well, write a list of what you want the thought-form to do and how. For some matters, this will be very straightforward, but it will be a matter of setting limits and boundaries of its work for others. For example, you may wish to create an earth-type thought-form to protect a patch of land area outside while you are absent. Perhaps a small earthen man made of rock comes to mind or a wispy, swift communicating spirit who will watch an area unseen and tell you when something happens. Maybe a water spirit thought-form to guard against floods and negotiate with the water spirits in your absence would be more helpful. Animal-type thought-forms may also have many of these qualities and more, making them useful in guarding your home or sending protection to someone in need. There are many good animals to use as a basis for this, so think it through carefully.

Next, decide how long you want the thought-form to exist. A period of one to three months is a good starting point; when the time is up, the thought-form can be renewed or made again if you wish. Other thought-forms are made to serve a magical practitioner for their whole lives and may become cherished allies that have gathered much more energy, life, and skill over their time. However, the problem will always lie in the effective dissipation of such a being; left to run loose after a practitioner passes, they have been known to cause repeated trouble. They are sometimes the cause of hauntings, poltergeist activity, and other negative events. For this reason, effective boundaries and stringent spiritual/magical hygiene are essential! We must be ethical and take responsibility for what we do, lest some other practitioner years from now must clean up after us. I personally have had to clean up the messes left by now-deceased magical workers more than once, and the harm it caused rippled far and is now a stain on their spirits, one that endures into the otherworld, I'm sure.

When we are clear about what we want to make, why, and what we want it to do and how long we want it around, the next task is to gather something to serve as the spirit's home or symbolically represent its presence—a stone or some other object could work depending on what is right for its task, a bottle, or a box—many use the skull of an animal for this purpose (I advise only ethically sourced) and place the thought-form within that. Whatever it is, see that it is strongly and effectively cleansed first—submerse it in running water or cleanse it with smoke or by another method.

After securing a home or symbol for it, you must decide on a name for it.

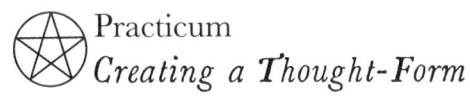

Practicum
Creating a Thought-Form

Before you begin, gather small bowls of earth and water, as well as a candle and some incense. When you are ready, create an appropriate magical space and light your candle and incense. I recommend creating a caim with strong boundaries so that the intentions remain strong and no other energies become unwittingly involved. Next, draw up the serpent energy from the earth, the living light within the land, into your body with deep slow breaths. Let your mind calm and begin to form your familiar.

You have already decided its shape and form, so now in your inner vision give it shape and finer detail. For example, say you chose a gruff badger-type being to guard the home and serve as a reassuring, earthy presence at the threshold in front of the right people. Perhaps now you'd like to specify that the being can change size and become ferocious and terrifying to the unwelcome until they feel so uncomfortable and afraid of *something* that they leave at speed. See the badger's thick, bristly hair, its sharp black claws good for digging the earth. See its shining black eyes that tell you this being can be benevolent to the right people but is smart enough to know the welcome from the unwelcome. Envision the shape of its back and belly, its head in clear detail, the black and white stripes down its face and back, the clean animal smell, the huff of its breath, the gruff voice of its bark in the night.

As you visualise all these details, hold your hands open. Use your breath to send the energy up from the land to between your hands, forming the spirit's shape, sending more and more energy into it until you feel it grow powerful. Speak to it all the while, listing the work it is to do, how, and for how long. List any relevant boundaries to its work and other details, including introducing it to its home. When it is ready, move the thought-form in your hands to the object and condense it, pushing and letting it flow into the object of its physical representation. Keeping your hands on it, continue to breathe and send the serpent energy from the earth into it until it feels right to stop.

When this stage is complete, place it over the bowl of earth and sprinkle some upon it, saying:

You are given life by the earth.

Then bring the object to the incense, wafting it through the smoke:

You are given life by the air.

Now bring it above the flame briefly and safely. Say:

You are given life by the fire.

Next move it over the bowl of water. Sprinkling a little upon it, say:

You are given life by the water.

Finally, hold it in your hands and draw it to you. Say:

I name you _____, and by my breath you are given life for the next _____ [duration of time].

Repeat this last line over and over until you feel it is done, letting a light trance overcome you and feeling a strong bond build between you and the thought-form.

When the work is done and your caim is taken down or released, either keep this object with you or place it somewhere suitable for it to do its work.

Take care to tune in to it regularly to see how it is faring and what it wants to convey. Of course, be open to receiving its messages randomly, should it need to immediately communicate with you. When you check in with it, you may feed it with more energy raised from the earth or place offerings before its object to feed its energy and help it do good work.

Make careful note of the date of when it should be dismantled; if it is to work in the long term, take steps to ensure you have someone who knows about it and is tasked to carry out your will should you be unable for any reason.

To dismantle or destroy it, call it to you and draw its energy from the object. Using cleansing smoke or running water, see it dissipate into nothing, thinning and fading and dissolving. As you do so, you may say the following over and over as you waft the smoke around the object and therefore the thought-form:

Your time is done and now you are nothing!

When steps are taken to dismantle it, a thought-form cannot stay together long without any source of life or energy; it lives only on what you have given it. Accordingly, you must be clear in your mind to see it truly and cleanly ended. When it is fully dissipated, place your hands fully on the earth and let the land take any lingering energy. Afterwards, you may wash the object in running river water or sea water for a time.

Familiars

The practice of keeping animal spirits as familiars differs from both that of living animals and thought-forms, in that an animal spirit has its own living spirit intelligence along with its own agency and judegement. That said, they can be far more intelligent and creative than living animals, able to work independently on sophisticated, complex tasks. Keep in mind that the relationship with this kind of familiar is more of an equal partnership than with the others—an animal spirit may disagree with you about your course of action or do something in your interests that you haven't asked for. It can also decide to leave if the relationship has served its time or purpose.

⛤ Practicum
Gaining an Animal Spirit Familiar

This practice can be performed indoors but is best performed on the land at a suitable power point or a physical crossroads if you can do so uninterrupted. Take an offering of food and a single candle.

Sitting on the land or in your indoor ritual space, settle yourself. Breathing deeply, draw up the serpent energy, the light from the land, until it surrounds you and you feel a sense of connection and deep calm descend upon you.

Light your candle. Gazing into its flames, feel yourself falling into a light trance state as you call out your intention to gain an animal spirit familiar to work with you. Repeat these or other suitable words over and over until they form a soft chant to focus you:

I call you, come to me, familiar!
Animal kin, spirit of wild, the company of the wise, I call to you!
I call to you, familiar spirit!
I call you, wise creature!
Come to me now!

Give the process plenty of time. Let your eyes settle upon the flame or close completely. If you are in a place on the land, let your spirit wander and be aware of what may come to you at this meeting place between the worlds. If you are indoors, travel to such a place in your inner vision and call to your future animal familiar from there.

When an animal spirit comes to you, you may question and converse with it, keeping in mind that you need only accept it if it feels right to you. This is a hard thing to describe that must be experienced in practice. You may find several animal spirits come or none, in which case you must repeat this over and over until you are effective.

Once you find one that feels right, you may or may not be given a name to use or a clear method for calling it, but often these aren't necessary due to its independent nature—it will know when you call in your intention and inner vision, feeling your pull across the web of creation. Feed this familiar regularly by sending it gifts of energy or giving it offerings. Ask it what it likes and how often it would like to receive—you may find you need to make a regular agreement with it.

Look out on the land in your daily or nightly travels for signs of its physical presence. Take sightings of the kind of animal it is—even if these are random on TV or your phone—as a friendly wave or communication from them. Check in on it in vision often, and when you engage in magical practice or are just going about your day, call to it to accompany you. See it in your inner vision alongside you wherever you go.

Familiars as Allies

Animal spirit familiars have much in common with shamanic power animals or the animal-formed tutelary spirits of our old Celtic clans. Although these spirits can guide, advise, and empower us, the relationship must be respected for it to be fruitful. Do not ignore a familiar's advice, even when it refers to something you haven't asked about. The advantages of an animal spirit familiar is its ability to be there for you and have a perspective beyond your own. Think of theirs as eyes watching your back rather than only looking where you tell it to. Such allies are invaluable and should be treasured. Unlike a thought-form, these do no harm if the person dies or forgets about them, and over a practitioner's life many animal spirits may come and go according to the needs and interests inherent in the work, but all should be appreciated as cocreators in a strong magical practice.

Fairies and Elves

The relationship between wise women and cunning folk with the fairies is a long one of great antiquity. Native Celtic magical practices often rely on a strong relationship with the otherworld and the spirits of the landscape. These can take many forms, including nature spirits, fairies, the tutelary gods of the area and those overseeing the bloodlines of local families. Although fairies are known as dangerous beings often humanoid in form but immortal and immoral, the reality is more subtle than this suggests. Much of our knowledge of fairies in folklore is seen through a Christian lens where the fairies' innate ambiguity raises fears and mistrust of what are otherwise key allies in the psychic landscape. And declaring fairies "evil" and "immoral" raises the question—are humans innately good and helpful? What about other beings?

Is a tree or a river a moral being? When dealing with powerful, intelligent spirit nations, we must respect their ways and separate our human-centric and often Christianised morality from their innate connection to the earth and values, usually centring far more around a holistic view of all living things that sits slightly outside of our sense of time. Although these beings are powerful and not driven by the motivations most humans share, that doesn't make them bad or evil any more than a rainstorm or any other kind of spirit we may encounter is. They are operating on a far, far, wider perspective than we.

It is this difference in perspective that makes fairy connection so useful to the human magical practitioner. The fairies are curious about our position in time and space, and we may gain a great deal from their far closer communion with the soul of the land and the fiery serpent power of the earth. Bear in mind that there is no danger in fairy connection—far from it! But there is great power and wisdom to be gained that for some may outweigh the risk.

We know many of the historical witches prosecuted in the Scottish witch trials disclosed having fairy helpers, making deals with, or being allied with the king or queen of the fairies or the king and queen of "elfhame." Such pacts and close relationships were considered (by the prosecutors at least) to be a sign of evil influence almost akin to devil worship. Some of these witches were quite open about practising maleficium, presuming we believe their testimony. But there is little overt evidence that such fairies were wanting people to practice evil magic—the average relationship non-magical workers had with the fairies or their elven kin was one of fear and cautious respect wherein their danger was mitigated by a series of careful taboos. Instead, it seems that fairies and elves were feared but also approached when in need for their support, just as the wise women and cunning folk were who mediated their relationship with their nearest human communities.

In Ireland the situation between the Sidhe—which we now call by the name fairies—was slightly different, most likely because the relationship between magical workers and the church was different. Whilst critical of magical workers, the Catholic authorities in Ireland did not persecute them with much enthusiasm, and an uneasy truce endured between the fairy faith and the Catholic church. There were very few witch trials in Ireland compared to the witch hunting frenzy suffered by those in Scotland. Wales was equally muted in their pursuit and persecution of witches, largely due to the differing forms of Christianity in each locale. In Ireland, the wise woman or fairy doctor garnered great respect but was rarely thought to perform malicious magic, though they were feared and commanded deep respect. When such suspicions arose in Wales, it seldom resulted in prosecution let alone execution as in Scotland.

Fairies in our native magical and folkloric traditions are a far cry from the saccharine confections of the New Age or the Victorian children's illustrations that dominate our common understanding of them. In contexts magical and folkloric, they are often of or close to human height, and much has been made of their ability to walk among us unrecognised. While some fairies from folklore are smaller than humans, they are still described as three or four feet in height—the tiny and winged fairies are rarely if ever seen at all. Sometimes they do not even have any form except the dancing lights known as will o' the wisps seen alone in wild places after dark. Sometimes fairies are solitary beings, but traditionally they were said to live in highly organised social groups with a king and queen as their leaders.

As already covered, they have a different morality and value system to humans and to pin the idea of good or bad upon them is to do them a great disservice and infantilises the seeker, denying the opportunity to broaden and deepen our sense of possibilities along with our magical and spiritual understanding. Fairies are traditionally connected to ancient sites and liminal spaces in the landscape as well as certain trees and other significant localities such as mountain tops, wells, and remote lakes. They are best understood as a landscape's native spirit intelligences, civilised and sentient in their own way—and powerfully so. We should consider them alongside the native spirit peoples of other cultures rather than see them through the lens of popular culture or post-Christian morality.

A wise woman may work with a fairy for many reasons: Often they are an excellent source of magical training and grant access to considerable power. Historically in Scotland such relationships were formalised with magical pacts between the wise woman and the fairy spirit. In Ireland, the connection seems to be more a social one, and the accounts from England and Wales are also varied. That said, the relationship is always carefully choreographed by various taboos and strict etiquette.

The Sidhe and the Alfar

As already discussed, many healers and wise women were said to gain their powers and knowledge through being in service to the Fairy King or Queen. Allegiance to the Fairy Queen is most common, as the Fairy King is perhaps more often concerned with the initiation of the seeker and the guardianship of the land and its traditions, although these are never hard and fast rules. Often in Scotland, the queen is known as the Queen of Elphame, which can be understood as similar to "fairy" but not quite the same. "Elf" or "elfphame"/"elfhame" are from the Lowland Scots and Northern English traditions, and the term is used specifically in the Lowland Scots ballads of Tam Lin and Thomas the Rhymer, in addition to the Scottish witch trials where numerous people accused of witchcraft were said to be in league with her. The roots of "elfphame," "elf home," and "elf" are drawn from the Germanic, Saxon, and Norse parts of Scots and British heritage, which are particularly strong in Scotland and Northern England.

In Ireland we do not find the term "elf"; rather we have the Irish *Sidhe*, "the people of the mounds," among others, such as the banshees, leprechauns, and pookas. In Wales are the *Tylwyth Teg* ("the fair family") as well as the Bwbachod (similar to household brownies), the Gwragedd Annwn (female fairies of the lakes and streams) and the Ellyllon, which are more akin to the elves of Scotland and England, among others.

The term "fairy" is used to refer to all the above and more but could just as easily be understood to refer to none of them at all, as it denies their individual natures and cultures. The word "fairy" itself is drawn from the Early Modern English *faerie*, meaning "realm of the fays." The term "faerie" derives from the Old French *fay* or *fae*, itself a derivation from the vulgar Latin *fata*, "the fates," as in the supernatural goddesses who could foretell the future and knew the fate, life, and death of every person.[36]

In Old French romances, the fay were women skilled in magic and healing or cursing potions, similar to the wise women and fairy doctors of Celtic traditional magic. As you can see, the history and meaning of the word has

---

36. "Fairy," Online Etymological Dictionary, accessed February 27, 2024, https://www.etymonline.com/search?q=fairy.

moved from grander mythological connotations and is intimately entwined with those who work with them as well as the fairy spirits themselves.

The king, queen, and indeed any fairies we may read about are not singular beings—they are titles we may find in our local area if we are allowed to encounter them. Equally, they are individuals who are also hive beings, living in far closer connection with the land and each other than we can comprehend from our human perspective. When we meet them or seek them out, we must do so as beings living as closely with our landscape as possible, holding in our hearts a strong sense of our vast interconnectedness so as to align ourselves with their frequency and values, for the best results.

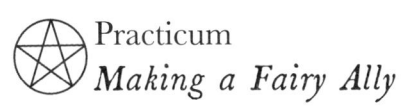

Practicum
Making a Fairy Ally

We may seek a fairy ally in our inner vision, but working on the land at a fairy site can be very powerful if it is possible.[37] In Britain and Ireland there are numerous fairy sites—most commonly fairy forts, the archaeological remains of Iron Age hillforts and smaller Norman castles. In other places, fairy sites may be ancient burial mounds or a sacred lone thorn tree. Ancient springs, wells, and standing stones are also good for fairy contact, as of course are crossroads. However, fairies in various forms are known across the world and have long been considered to have travelled to the United States accompanying emigrating families. Ancient woods, wells, or simply empty crossroads may be the most suitable and practical places for this work. Take heed of local folklore and older precolonial traditions when considering where to seek fairy contact—above all, fairies demand respect not only for themselves but for the earth and the ancestors. If there is traditional lore about the site to guide you, familiarise yourself with it in advance, taking care to follow its rules as well as your intuition.

When intending to connect with a fairy, prepare an offering. The most common is food and drink laid upon a small white cloth but bowls of fresh water or the ability to play an instrument or sing a song are also suitable. As well, be prepared to sit out in nature at your chosen site for a vigil of a significant length of time, perhaps even overnight. Wear sensible footwear,

---

37. Additional discussion and practices on fairies can be found in my book *Wild Magic* (Llewellyn, 2020).

bring rain gear, and take all common-sense precautions. Such matters may not seem magical, but any good animist who has spent time out in the countryside can tell you sensible gear helps you do better magical and spiritual work than a fancy but rain-soaked cloak any day.

If possible, perform this rite on one of the cross-quarter days: Imbolc, Bealtaine, Lughnasadh, or Samhain. However, really any day works if the fairies are willing. Travel to your chosen site well before sundown. Once there, seek a place that feels powerful in which you may sit in uninterrupted privacy with suitable shelter if necessary. After preparing your space and attending to practical matters, sit in deep peaceful connection with the land, meditating and chanting as the sun goes down. As dusk gathers, lay out your offerings and call aloud to the four airts, the spirit kin you met when spying the four directional roads to aid you. Next, call upon the powers of place and the spirits of the site where you sit to aid you. Finally, call upon the fairies, the Sidhe, or the elves to send an ally forth for you to work with. Try the following or similar words:

Fairy spirits of this place,
Great ones of the mound, dwellers of the hollow hills:
I call to you!
Send an ally forth to me to teach me of your ways
In goodness and with kind and honourable hospitality!

As you sit on the land, seek to merge your spirit with that of the earth with your breath and innate connection, entering a watchful yet light trance state. Take heed of what you hear, feel, or see, including any physical sensations or flashes of vision. In time, a fairy being may approach you, but do not expect to see it so much as feel it.

It may be that this rite may take several attempts to be successful; be aware and take heart that each and every time will deepen your connection with fairy and the land. This connection on its own will be deeply fruitful and make what you gain all the more significant when you finally are successful.

Practicum
Spirit Flight: Meeting the Fairy King and Queen

Meeting the fairy king and queen by any name and in any of the various Celtic and British traditions we may know them from can be a powerful experience. However, forming a relationship with them must be the result of careful prior consideration on our part, as they may demand our allegiance. Even if it sounds or we believe it to be beneficial for us, thought and discernment are required. If you are given such an offer during this spirit flight, I advise waiting until a later date and asking many questions before you even consider agreeing. Consider this exercise simply a first step on a longer road.

Wait until midnight on a full moon. Prepare your sacred space as you wish but see that your space is tidy, attractive, and ordered lest you displease them. Bring with you a single candle and an offering of butter, honey, or ale and place it before the candle as a gift just for them that you may place outside after the rite.

Sitting at the centre of your cairn or sacred space, breathe slowly, drawing up the light from the land, feeling its serpent current rising within you. Let your vision soften as you stare at the candle flame. Voice aloud your intent:

King and queen of the fairies, may I meet thee and enter your court this night as a respectful guest.

Your sense of where you are fades, and you see yourself stood by a wooden gate with a path of pale chalky earth weaving through long grass ahead of you. It is twilight. The gate is the boundary between the mortal human world and theirs. Pause and be conscious before crossing over.

Follow the path as it winds up a gentle hillside. The stars above you begin to come out and glitter brightly above you. Gradually the climb grows steeper, and you feel the distance from the world of humans increase one step after the other as you enter a wild, quiet place of wind and heather.

Ahead of you a great mound rises up, silhouetted against the sky. As you approach it, you feel a change and a charge in the atmosphere. You hear the sound of people darting through the darkness around you. Pause a moment and bow your head in respect—you are entering a domain not for humankind. Next say in a clear voice:

People of the mounds, Fairy King and Queen: I come in respect and in friendship. Please may I enter?

Walk clockwise around the mound until you find an entrance, a low dolmen arch of three flat stones, one on either side and one above as a lintel. Is there light or darkness within? There may be a guardian at the door, which you must speak to and ask for admittance.

If you are able to enter, step within gently, one foot in front of the other. If you are not admitted, you must return another day and try again.

As you go deeper into the mound, you see light ahead and enter a vast cavern filled with light. Many beings of varied forms fill the cavern, and there is great activity and noise all around you. Before you go too far in, stop again to greet them respectfully.

In time, you will be led before the king and queen. They may take any form but are usually easy to identify. One will choose to speak with you: Take note of whether it is the king or the queen. The one who chooses to speak may indicate much about your magical path ahead and its nature.

Remember that this is the king and queen of the fairies nearest your physical location that is also on another layer of reality; there are many fairy kings and queens, all interconnected due to their very nature. They will already know much about you. You must be truthful and heart-led in your interactions with them. Be straightforward, even if you find them complex and puzzling in their conduct with you. To be true in nature and spirit is your best course of action.

After a time, you will be dismissed. Take special care to return to your mortal self along the same route you took to reach the mound, this time in reverse.

Fairies and the Dead

The Celtic otherworld and the realms of fairy have long been associated with the dead. In rural areas particularly in Ireland, people often saw their dead relatives dwelling with or accompanying the fairies, and some certainly believed that they themselves would join the fairies when they died. Several historical wise women in Ireland, including the famous Biddy Early, were taught and advised by dead relatives with their dealings with fairies and the deceased person would often mediate with the fairies on their behalf.[38] Seers and other magical workers of the Celtic traditions were often presumed to go to the fairies when they died and dwell with them in one of their hollow hills.

A folk witch or Celtic wise woman often works with the ancient honoured dead to deepen their communion with the earth, to draw advice and wisdom as well as help with supporting or healing the land or the people who dwell on it. The ancient honoured dead are those who not only lived long ago but who are honoured with special burial practices. In the British and Irish landscape, these places are often easy to identify as the Neolithic and Bronze Age burial cairns, as well as Iron Age burial sites often found at hillforts. Due to their status as sites of archaeological importance, they must be treated with great respect—they are ancestral sites in both the physical and energetic sense. We treat them as places where we honour the spirits *and* are stringent in doing no harm to the archaeology present.

Visiting these sites is certainly the best way to connect with the ancient honoured dead, but because their presence in the spirit world is as strong as on the physical plane, we are not limited to only visiting in person—we may also visit them in spirit, and when we have a strong connection to them, they are capable of visiting us, too! I have a strong family connection to the sites in the Boyne Valley in Ireland, and at times of need or if I haven't visited recently, it is quite common for me to suddenly feel the presence of my ancestors and the sites themselves as distinct energy beings.

When we are able to connect with the honoured ancient dead, we have the ability to grow our roots really deep, not only as magical practitioners seeking strong connection with the serpent forces of the earth but as humans. Such ancestors who dwell in the mounds are often ones who have chosen to remain in a state of in-betweenness; they are in connection to the earth and the spirit realm but also close enough to living humans to advise and support those who come after them. It is a great honour to connect with such beings. Other honoured ancient dead have chosen to stay as protectors of a site or for another reason, and these too are souls in service to something greater than themselves that should be honoured, even if they are fierce in their

---

38. "Biddy Early," Clare Library, accessed February 28, 2024, https://www.clarelibrary.ie/eolas/coclare/people/biddy.htm.

protectiveness. Great healing can come to a landscape if we honour its spirit protectors.

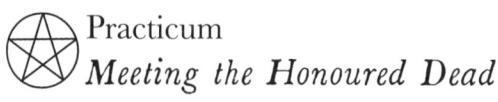

⛤ Practicum
Meeting the Honoured Dead

This practice is similar to seeking a fairy ally in that the best way to do it is prolonged and attentive time spent on the land. However, it can also be performed at a distance with regular attunement and connection rather than a long vigil.

Before setting out, learn all you can about your chosen site: Look into its archaeology, folklore, general history, and topography—anything that may be of use. Research is particularly important if you are only visiting in spirit, but it is still important if you are visiting in person. Next, prepare a suitable offering: ale, honey, or butter are often good for ancestors in Britain and Ireland. What you offer may be adapted with sensible changes to sites and ancestors in other countries so long as all relevant cultural sensitivities and rules for visitors are heeded.

Visit your chosen site just before either dusk or dawn. After a few minutes of silently centring yourself, lay out your offering and call to the spirits of the four airts, those beings you found upon each road. Ask them for their assistance in seeking an ancestral teacher.

Using great care and politeness, call out and ask that one of the honoured ancient dead attend to you so that you may learn a little of their wisdom.

Sitting in a quiet spot that feels right, calmly settle yourself as you await a response. Let your vision soften and a light trance come over you. You may then see or feel certain presences around you, and it's common for a site to have more than one ancestor spirit present. If there are many, don't be afraid of asking one in particular to come forwards or that the others step back, so that you can all understand each other better.

If you are visiting in spirit, you may find you wander the site in your inner vision and come across another being there who will converse with you. If you are physically present, pay particular attention to how everything feels in your body. Allow yourself to move around the site if called to do so. Be open to the spirits communicating with you in all sorts of ways. Strive to be as present and connected as possible, taking care to feel in connection with the earth and the serpent energy as much as possible up and down your whole body, breathing consciously.

Illustration 9: Fairy Burial Mound at Stoney Littleton

Ancestor Box

If you are able to do so whilst doing absolutely no harm to a site, open your senses to see if you can receive something from it to take with you to maintain the connection. However, *never* take a stone from a cairn or a piece of earth from a fairy hill or other burial site of the honoured dead—you will pay sorely for doing so, and these are huge taboos! What you may do is look for things such as a feather or a twig fallen from a tree given as a gift. Additionally, *never* dig holes for soil or any other reason, and do not light fires there. Honour these sites and their spirits by facing the little inconveniences inherent in ethically visiting sacred archaeological sites and acting as one of their loving custodians. If nothing like a twig or a feather reveals itself, do not look around for something, anything to take—the spirits will be watching, and you will endanger yourself severely. Instead, ask the spirits to be present in a photo so you can remember them and tune in again from afar. When you can, print the photo and keep it in a special box or bag used only for connecting with the honoured ancient dead of that site, together with herbs that honour the spirits there, such as meadowsweet, vervain, or dried hawthorn berries. If you are never able to visit in person, print a photo of the site from elsewhere and use it as your entrance to visit in spirit. Again, honour the spirits of the place with offerings of herbs.

At regular intervals and especially at Samhain, place an offering of food and drink for the ancient honoured dead next to the box. And if you are able, visit them in person.

Part Two
A Cottage Grimoire
*Spells and Charms for
Cunning Folk and Wild Witches*

In this section is a large collection of spells and charms that I have found helpful over the years. Some of these are very old and are presented in their original forms, while many others are adaptations of my own, just as I'm sure they were adapted by countless others over the years, to be suitable both for the world today and my own ethics and uses. I've kept many of these in notebooks and my own records for decades so the origins of some are now lost, but I've listed their sources where possible to encourage you to honour their cultural and historical roots. Other spells and charms are ones of my own invention, guided and inspired by my allies and familiars. Let them all be a storehouse for you to dip into whenever you need and inspiration to support you in developing your own spells, charms, and practices. I also include recipes for potions, powders, and incenses that have stood the test of time. Remember that none of these things are written in stone—you should use a bit of intuition and a bit of experience when you want to adapt what you find to yourself so that you can use what you have or finesse what's there for your own needs.

Chapter 10
Candle Spells

Candles and flame have always been used in ritual and magical settings—they may provide suitable lighting for a ritual and be constructed so their virtues align with the purpose of the rite or the spell, or they may be the main instrument of the magic itself. A candle is transformative in its very nature, changing one thing—the wax, wick, and any other ingredients, directly into flame, into light and heat. A good quality candle will burn down with no trace left, making it perfect for magic. It can take the virtues and energies contained within it and sublimate them into a noncorporeal or spirit form. In this way, it can send a powerful wave of whatever we choose out into the spirit realm that in turn filters back into the physical world. This can be creative, drawing in what we desire, or it can be destructive, transforming something negative or no longer useful into something positive or even returning it to the sender. Candle spells can also send out healing by the same logic—by sending healing virtues into the flames, they may send that light of healing into another as the candlelight is extinguished, and so on. The possibilities are vast for this simple form of magic, which is why it is so beloved and practiced so widely.

What follows is not a complete or exhaustive survey of candle magic; it is too large a subject for here, but what you find here should provide some guidance and instruction on producing some of your own candle spells with a simple overview of the possibilities.

Practicum
A Candle for the Spirits

This is perhaps the simplest form of candle magic you can do: The simple lighting of a candle to invoke your spirit allies or gods. Always use the best quality candles you can for ritual or magical purposes so that your intention is clear and not sullied by poor materials. For this exercise, I encourage you to use a pure white candle or a natural beeswax one so that there is no other element woven into the work via the candle's colour or scent.

Set your candle somewhere safe in a ritual setting, and make sure you are calm and focused. Taking up a fresh match, light the candle and call in your intended spirit. For example:

I call to you now helpful spirit, ally of mine, aid me with my spirit work here tonight.

What you say would presumably address a spirit you have already worked with, but you can use it to call in any helpful spirit. As the candle is lit, breathe slowly and spend some time resting your eyes upon the flame, maintaining awareness of how you have brought something into physical existence. With it, you have called a spirit into this realm—a hybrid being really, a flame spirit and the helpful spirit you called.

You can extend this practice to calling in your gods, animal familiars, ancestors, and so on; the key is in your intention and focus. This differs widely from merely lighting a candle and can be a powerful practice on its own. You can sit with the candle flame, meditate in the presence of the being you have called, and even ask it to advise you through your inner vision or by observing the movements of the flame.

When it is time, thank the being you have called and snuff the candle out rather than blow it out. Using your breath to extinguish can give something life and would set the being free of its mooring on the flame with potentially chaotic and even dangerous results.

Types of Candles

There are many types of candles that can be used for magic; good quality ones of various appropriate colours for spells are a good foundation. These candles can be anointed with any oils and herbs—oil first will help the herbs stick, so individual candle choices can be further personalised for a specific task. And while it's good to anoint and wrap your candles in herbs, it isn't essential—think of it as a useful and powerful addition if circumstances warrant or allow it. Ultimately, a plain candle can do everything a fancy coloured and anointed candle can do with enough intention and focus used with it. You can also buy or make flat sheets of candle wax that are rolled into candles. These allow for more personalisation and encasing herbs or written charms within the candle itself, which I like.

Of course, you can also make your own candles, giving you total freedom in personalisation: materials, colours, and anything you wish to add such as herbs, oils, and other details such as charms, written spells, and suitably sized physical items. Powerful personal ingredients such as hair or blood can also be added if you are making your own candles. The only consideration is to make sure the ratio between other items and the wax itself is still appropriate for it to burn in a steady and predictable manner. The more you add, the more wax you will need to cover them properly. Wicks can also be added which can be soaked and infused with things like herbal oils tisanes or other elements.

Candles and Other Correspondences

Candles can be separated into different colours for different purposes that are usually related to planetary or other correspondences. The time and day of the week that the spell is performed can also add extra power to the spell, as can the time of year. The herbs and oils used to anoint the candle can also had extra power to the spell, aligning it further with your focus.

Candle Colours

White: Purity, protection, peace; Mondays, the moon

Lavender: Intuition, dignity, spiritual shielding, peace

Purple: Spirituality, intuition, clairvoyance, divination; power; Neptune

Light blue: Clear communication, peace

Blue: Meditation, tranquillity; communication, expression

Deep blue: Prosperity, wealth; Thursdays; Jupiter

Green: Healing; prosperity; love and friendship; Friday; Venus

Light green: Mother earth; growth; luck, blessings; planet Earth

Yellow: Clairvoyance; communication; optimism; intellect, study; Wednesday; Mercury

Orange: Strength; prosperity and success, joy; resolving legal issues; Sunday; the sun

Pink: Emotional love, harmony, romance, friendship

Bright red: Self-love; friendship; goddess connection; blood/menstruation magic; Tuesday; Mars

Red: Love, passion, courage, sexuality

Black: Absorbs negative energy, honouring the dead, Saturday, Saturn

Silver: New ideas, money, psychic ability, purity, Monday, the moon

Gold: Sovereignty, wealth, inner knowledge, divinity, Sundays, the sun

Brown: Stability; loyalty; earthing; garden magic; pet protection as well as animals and familiars; planet Earth

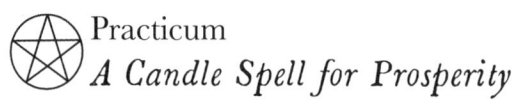

Practicum
A Candle Spell for Prosperity

On a Thursday, Jupiter's day, select a candle in deep blue, the colour relating the virtues of the planet Jupiter. Inscribe the candle, using a knife or cocktail stick, with the symbol for Jupiter and the symbol of the currency wherever you are in the world (e.g., £, $, €, and so on) and anoint it with frankincense oil. Surround the candle-holder with a circle of basil leaves and as many high-value coins as you have on hand.

Striking a fresh match, light the candle and say:

I call upon you Jupiter, aid in my magics and draw prosperity to me, bring me wealth, money and abundance! I call to you—may my spell be true!

Repeat the words over and over, eyes resting on the flame. Hold out your hands and project your intention into the flame. Keep this going for as long as feels right to you, allowing the candle to burn down completely. If you must pause the spell after a while, snuff it out and repeat the whole process the next Thursday, relighting it until the candle has burnt to nothing.

⛤ Practicum
A Candle Spell for Banishing

On a Saturday, Saturn's day, take a black candle and inscribe upon it what you wish to be rid of or the name of the person you believe has been attacking you. Anoint the candle with raw garlic or garlic oil and surround it in a circle of salt so that the negative energy drawn to it cannot escape.

Be clear beforehand what you wish to say and how you wish to verbally direct the magic. For example:

I banish my anger now, I let my anger go, let me gain knowledge from it, and transform it now to inform my life with wisdom so it need not return! Anger be gone, I transform you now! Anger be gone I transform you now!

If it is a person you wish to be rid of, you could say the following or similar:

I banish you, [name of person], from my life now. May you do no more harm! I banish you now! I banish you now!

If someone has done you harm, use your inner vision to gather up the energy of that harm from yourself and your life. Using your hands, direct it into the flame to be transformed. You can speak to the flame and pour out your feelings, if you like, seeing the emotional energy eaten by the flame and transformed.

Again, let the candle burn down in a single sitting if possible; if not, remember to snuff it out instead of blowing, and repeat as often as needed on other Saturdays.

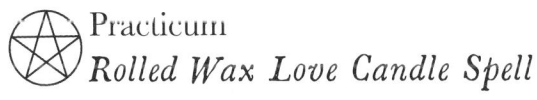

⛤ Practicum
Rolled Wax Love Candle Spell

On the day ruled by Venus, Friday, take one sheet of red or pink candle wax, a wick, some dried rose petals, and a ritual knife or cocktail stick to inscribe the wax. You could also add several drops of rose oil on the inside of the roll.

After you have prepared your ritual space with all the practical elements of your task taken care of, such as assembling your materials and arranging a suitable surface, take your wax sheet. After softening it with a hairdryer if necessary, inscribe the word "love" gently into the wax using your instrument, being careful not to cut all the way through the wax, maintaining your intent and focus. You may like to write the word several times (just once is perfectly fine as well) and if you'd like, include any additional designs or sigils. If you'd like to speak aloud, you could say something like, "I call love to me now" over and over as you inscribe.

Lay your rose petals across the sheet, adding some rose oil if you choose. Don't use so much that it will drastically affect how the candle burns—you only need enough to be able to roll the wax over it. Again, you may need to gently warm the wax first. As you do so, thank the roses and continue to chant "I call love to me now" to keep your focus. Next, gently but firmly roll the candle wax around the wick. Making sure the roll is tight, keep going until the wax is completely rolled with the rose petals within it. At this stage, you can use a hairdryer to melt the ends to seal it all in or leave it according to your design.

If you'd like, as your final step, soften the exterior of the candle again to anoint it with rose-scented almond oil and roll in loose rose petals; the warmth of the wax and oil will be needed for the petals to stick, making this more of an art than a science. Remember that the best results are always a result of experimentation.

Store the candle somewhere cool and dry; I like to wrap candles in waxed paper as well. When it is time to light it, ask the flame spirit to bring and surround you and your environment with love. Remember to never leave any candle unattended. When you are finished, use a snuffer and relight as necessary.

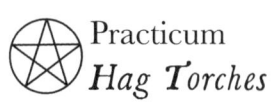

Practicum
Hag Torches

Hag torches are flaming torches made from dried mullein stalks. These large flowering plants have tall, statuesque stalks and seed heads that, when dried, can be coated in beeswax and used as outdoor candles, making them excellent for outdoor rites

First, gather dried stalks. Mullein is both easy to grow and is easily found growing wild, making it simple to forage in your area if it grows there. Gather the stalks by cutting with scissors a foot or two from the dead flower head depending on its condition, and gently shake it to disperse its seeds to grow in another year. Mullein is a biennial plant, which means it will not flower until its second year, so take care to leave any first-year plants growing at its base so you can use them next year.

Hang the mullein stalk and seed-head upside down somewhere to dry with plenty of air so that it is bone-dry before use. If it's gathered on a dry sunny day, you may find it is ready to use quite soon after collecting.

Illustration 10: Hag Torches

Prepare any corresponding herbs, spices, resins, or other materials you would like to add to the wax to decorate the torch. These can be aligned with your magical purposes, seasonal themes, or for their visual or aromatic qualities. Some spices can add natural colour to the wax, such as turmeric for yellow, paprika for fiery red. Charcoal or ashes, perhaps from a ritual fire, can be powdered and added to create black or grey wax.

Next, prepare a double boiler to gently melt your beeswax. Make sure whatever pot you use is deep enough for dipping your mullein into or else you will need a clean paintbrush (one to two inches wide) to brush the wax onto the mullein in layers. When the wax has melted, add any other materials, herbs, charcoal, and so on, stirring to distribute evenly. Take care with adding anything, as the wax will be very hot. At this stage, you might like to chant or intone prayers of intentions you wish to add to your torches, perhaps gently stirring or visualising any symbols or the energy you are putting into it as you do so. Once you are done, remove the wax from the heat so that it is not bubbling but still runny. Either drip or paint the wax onto your mullein seed heads using the paintbrush. Place each seed head gently on waxed paper to cool, or hang them somewhere safe until the wax has completely cooled and dried. Wrap carefully in more waxed paper and store them in a box (they are fragile) until you are ready to use them.

When lit, the mullein hag torch will burn at roughly one inch per hour, but this can vary. Position it so that any spitting from added ingredients and any remaining seeds can do no harm; if you carry it lit, make sure it is at arm's length.

Chapter 11
Healing Spells

A key part of folk magic and the wise woman's craft is healing, the curing of illness or injury in people or animals. This has a long-standing and venerable tradition across northern Europe, and we are fortunate that so much lore has survived. There are many similarities in practice across Britain and Ireland with variations in themes, so there is ample space to follow tradition and yet update and adjust to meet our needs today.

Of course, when performing any healing spells, we should be sensible and see them as a support and accompaniment to traditional Western medicine and first aid—*not* as replacements. The following is a selection of healing spells to explore for yourself.

Practicum
To Cure Warts

This West Country cure is local to me. Get a single long piece of straw from the field and tie a knot in it. Without speaking, pass it over the wart several times back and forth in silence before placing it down on the ground. If you have multiple warts, repeat this multiple times, one piece of straw per wart. When you have finished, bury the straw in the earth. As they rot and break down, the warts will disappear.

Here is another, also from the West Country.

Cut an elder stick and cut a notch within it. Touch the notch to the wart, one notch per wart. As you do this, remain silent throughout and bury the stick in the earth.

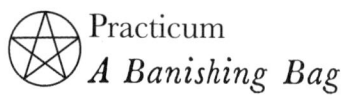

⛤ Practicum
A Banishing Bag

Take a stone and place it against the site of any illness—one stone per symptom or site on the body. Hold the stone and say:

You shall take this illness from me now!

As you speak, let it draw away what ails you. Wrap the stone in a cloth tie into a pouch or bag, or place it in a cardboard box. At the dark or waning moon, bury it at a crossroads.

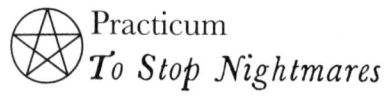

⛤ Practicum
To Stop Nightmares

A hag stone tied about the neck with red thread will protect the wearer from nightmares and all malicious spirits.

Shoe Magic

There is a lot of apotropaic shoe magic found across the United Kingdom, especially with regards to burying single shoes in a home's walls and chimney stack. They are often found in the north or resting on the chimney ledge within the hearth. Shoes were once expensive and have always been deeply personal objects that carry a lot of a person's energy. As such, they function well as spirit traps—any ill wishing sent to an individual and entering the house will find the shoe and mistake it for the person they have come to attack, thus leaving the actual person alone. The majority of shoes found as protection objects in old houses are children's shoes, showing the practice was considered particularly powerful for children, though the shoe can belong to anyone in the household and can be any type of shoe. Those who find old shoes usually leave them alone, lest it break the protection over the house.

Practicum
Shoe Spell for Protection

To protect yourself or your family from any specifically directed ill will, gather one old shoe per person, the older and more worn the better. Taking each shoe in turn, name them aloud as the person they represent and then wrap them in a black cloth. You may add iron nails or salt if you wish by placing them in the shoes or in the wrapped cloth alongside them.

When each shoe is wrapped, place them in a hidden space around your home. Some people in old houses have hidden cupboards behind their chimneys, others are able to brick up the shoes in a space made for this purpose when doing work on the house. If these options aren't available, they can be hidden in the loft, at the back of the airing cupboard, or any other place where they are likely to remain undisturbed. Such malicious magics will then be sent to the shoes rather than the person.

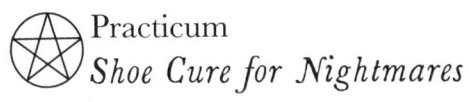

Practicum
Shoe Cure for Nightmares

An old West Country charm against nightmares and spirit visitations in the night is to place the shoes at the foot of the bed, with one shoe's toes pointing one way and the other shoe pointing in the opposite direction to confound the spirits and disturb their ability to locate you.

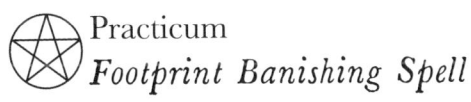

Practicum
Footprint Banishing Spell

To banish someone who is troubling you or is unwelcome, scatter some garlic and salt—or better still, some homemade banishing powder—on their footprints. As you do so, mutter unheard, "Be gone! Be gone! Be gone!" until you feel you have sent sufficient will into your intention.

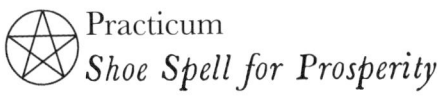

Practicum
Shoe Spell for Prosperity

To draw prosperity, place fresh basil leaves in your shoes so that you draw up the riches and abundance from the earth with every step.

⬟ Practicum
A Sciatica Charm

Variations of this are found across the United Kingdom, especially Scotland. "Boneshave" is a South West name for sciatica.

Take a straight stick the length of your body to a straight stretch of river. Lie down with the stick lengthways parallel between you and the water so the three of you are three straight parallel lines.

Then recite:

Boneshave right

Boneshave straight

As the water runs by the shave

Good for boneshave [39]

⬟ Practicum
Black Thread Healing Charm for Small Children

Originally this West Country charm local to my area calls for holding a baby in the waters of a spring, but I would obviously stress caution and great care with this and ultimately wouldn't recommend it. I see no reason why a small child cannot be held alongside the water or a shallow spring so the flow of the water may still take the illness or negative energy away without any danger or discomfort to the child. This spell can also be used on adults and vulnerable elders if all sensible steps and adaptations are applied. It can also be changed to remove sorrow, fear, upset, anxiety, and so on instead of illness. Simply change the words and intentions to suit.

Sensible note: Obviously this charm is no substitute for medical assistance—always seek the advice of your doctor when caring for sick children. Take every care with children around the water, and see that they are kept warm and carefully dried immediately afterwards. Always consider if the magic you are doing is suitable for the child's overall well-being.

---

39. James Halliwell-Phillipps, "IX–Superstition–Rhymes," *Popular Rhymes and Nursery Tales (1820–89)*, 46, accessed online June, 7, 2024, https://www.gutenberg.org/cache/epub/35707/pg35707-images.html#ix-superstition-rhymes.

Take a length of black thread that is biodegradable. Holding one end, let it flow along in the water. Holding the child carefully, draw the black thread out of the water and swirl it around the child three times anticlockwise, saying:

Illness, begone
Illness, begone
Illness, begone

Let some of the water touch the child so the water takes away the illness—you could dip their feet in it if it is safe.

Anoint the child with a little of the water on their brow (only if you are 100 percent sure the water is clean, warm enough, and safe enough to drink!). Bless the water, drawing its life force to the child as you say:

May this child be blessed
May this child be blessed
May this child be blessed

Repeat this spell for three days in a row, best during a waning moon.

On the third day after swirling the thread around the child, drop the black thread into the water to take all the illness away from the child to dissolve. Thank the water spirits when you have finished.[40]

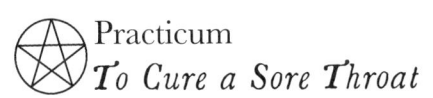

Practicum
To Cure a Sore Throat

Take a few pieces of birch twig. Hold them in your hand like a very small broom, and gently stroke your throat in an anticlockwise pattern to draw away the illness. When you are finished, bury the twigs.

---

40. This is my own adaptation of a traditional spell found from Devon to the Scottish Highlands. I base mine on the work of sixteenth-century fairy healer Andro Man from Scotland, who used black wool.

⛤ Practicum
To Cure Sprains and Broken Bones

This is known as a bone-to-bone spell that, while obviously no substitute for proper medical care, may speed healing. Indeed, there are many versions of bone-to-bone spells found all across Britain; their use likely goes back nearly a thousand years. This spell is best performed whilst directing energy into the wound and "stroking" gently along the wound or just above it in the direction where the healed bone or joint should be set. As you move your hands, say:

> *I will now this is the spell I intone*
> *Flesh to flesh and bone to bone*
> *Sinew to sinew and vein to vein*
> *Till each one shall be whole again*[41]

⛤ Practicum
Against Fatigue When Walking

Gather sprigs of fresh mugwort (*Artemesia vulgaris*), greeting the plant as a great friend when spied upon the wayside.

Place the leaves in your shoes so they rest against your skin when walking to ease fatigue and bless your journey. You will have fortune along the way and not become lost.

Caution: Do not use mugwort if you are pregnant or have menstrual issues.

⛤ Practicum
Against Weakness of the Eyes

Bramble has many magical uses; one of them is a tradition in which a person climbs under an arch of bramble rooted at both ends to drive illness or ill wishing away. Burning bramble has a similar effect. This spell to cure weakness of the eyes is also useful against all sorts of illness ill wishing and general weakness, depression, or lack of vitality—banishing whatever keeps the person away from a robust health and confidence.

---

41. I've known this verbal spell for more than thirty years and have made numerous adaptations to it, but there are a great many other versions and traditional variations found across the United Kingdom, especially in the South West.

Take several lengths of cut bramble and allow them to dry a little by hanging them somewhere sheltered. (If needed, they can be used green but will not burn as easily.)

When they are needed, set a good fire and thrust the ends of the brambles into the fire, allowing them to char and smoulder a little. Next, swipe and sweep the smoke in front of the eyes or around the person's body before sweeping down into the earth. Repeat this over and over until the bramble has been largely burnt down to what's held in your hand. A patch of leather or thick cloth may be used to hold the brambles safely to avoid the thorns.

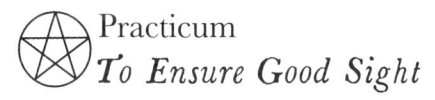

Practicum
To Ensure Good Sight

Fennel, rose, vervain, celandine, and rue
Do water make, which will the sight renew.

Make a tisane of these herbs in equal parts using fresh spring water gathered at the new moon. Once it has cooled completely, soak pads of fresh cotton in it and anoint the eyelids, resting the cotton on the eyes for a time each night for three nights.

Practicum
Against Numbness in a Limb

This charm using spittle has its roots in Irish fairy faith magic, where spit is often used to break a curse. In this tradition, spittle isn't considered dirty but rather the opposite—rich in the life force of the person it comes from, namely the wise woman or fairy doctor. Numbness is seen rather like a kind of theft of life force or soul in the fairy faith, and the so-called fairy stroke was a complaint often treated by fairy doctors and wise women, their symptoms bearing a strong resemblance to what we'd understand to be a regular stroke today. However, while in such serious circumstances immediate and urgent medical assistance should be sought first, lesser numbness such as that caused by poor circulation or sciatica, for example, can still be treated in this way.

With the affected limb in hand, spit upon it in the shape of an equal-armed cross along with the intention that whatever ails the person shall be driven off and the practitioner's life force act as a living thing of this earth that shields the afflicted until they recover.

Curses may be lifted also with spit onto the afflicted themselves, an object believed to be carrying the ill will, or the afflicted's footprint.

⛧ Practicum
Cure to Heal Fairy Darts or Elfshot

This cure is a traditional remedy for when a person has been attacked by the fairies. Fair attacks manifest in several ways: strokes of bad luck, pain in the side, persistent fatigue, or the cause of any ailment via divination and spirit contact. It is also good for use on livestock.

Take as many fairy darts or elfshot as you may have—usually understood archaeologically as flint arrowheads from the Neolithic era—or slingshot stones.[42] You could also use pieces of flint or beach pebbles as long as they feel right. Place them in some freshly drawn water (ideally from a spring) and leave under the moon. Then drink the water that has been imbued with the virtue of the darts so that they may no longer do harm.

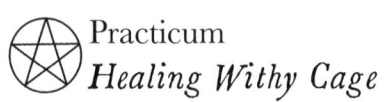

⛧ Practicum
Healing Withy Cage

A withy is a thin, whippy length of willow branch, usually a long, thin, fresh shoot cut in late spring when they are very flexible and about the thickness of a finger, although they can be selected and cut at any time.[43] The length used depends on their use. Withies grow rapidly and can be several feet long. A withy cage is a simple construction mostly used in the West Country to assist with healing serious injuries and broken bones. Obviously, it should only be used alongside medical attention. The willow is a powerful healing tree, rich in salicin, the active compound in aspirin that has powerful pain-relieving and anti-inflammatory properties. It is used here to house additional healing herbs and objects with an aim to strengthen their healing properties and encourage wholeness to make a complete healing bundle.

---

42. Marion Dowd, "Bewitched by an Elf Dart: Fairy Archaeology, Folk Magic and Traditional Medicine in Ireland," *Cambridge Archaeological Journal* 28, no. 3 (2018): 458.

43. An example can be found at the Museum of Witchcraft and Magic at Boscastle, Cornwall.

Take some thin lengths of willow about two feet long each (longer if desired) and bind them tightly top and bottom with red thread in such a way that there is some elasticity left and a space can be wedged between them in the centre where other herbs and written healing charms or other magical objects may be stored. Sing to the willow as you gather and tie, making your own healing charm that describes the person in need of healing and what is needed for them. Speak your intent clearly and name each object along with why you are including it as you place it within the bundle.

When it is complete, bind the whole thing tightly with red twine, to seal it in and place somewhere where it will not be disturbed until it is completely effective, at which time it may be gently dismantled.

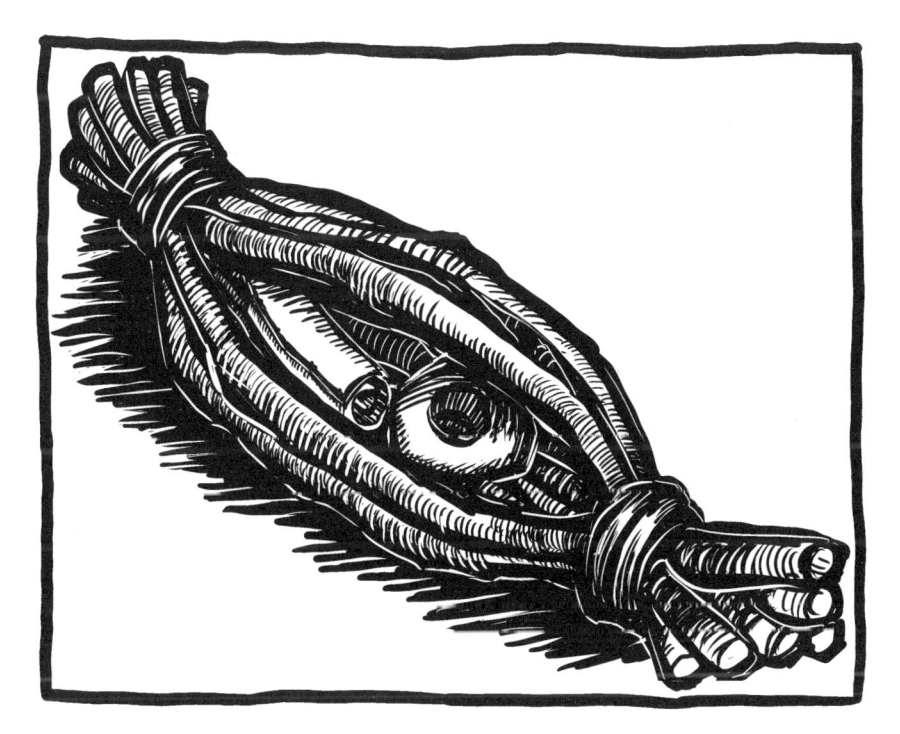

Illustration 11: Withy Cage

⛤ Practicum
Protection for Babies and Children

Gather a bunch of chamomile and cowslip together with ash or rowan leaves. Hang over the crib or beneath the bed (in a muslin bag if need be) to protect from illness or unwelcome spirits. You could also set a slip of rowan or ash wood under or around the bed.

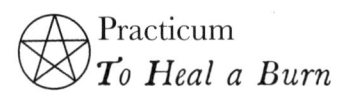

⛤ Practicum
To Heal a Burn

The practitioner places their hands above—not directly on—the burn after sensible medical assistance or first aid has been applied and recites:

> *Heat be gone*
> *Cool come in*
> *Heat be gone*
> *Cool come in*
> *Heat be gone*
> *Cool come in!*
> *All is healed all is well*
> *All is healed all is well*
> *All is healed all is well!*[44]

The Witch's Ladder

The witch's ladder is one form of a binding spell useful for all sorts of things from binding enemies to illness, to locking in blessings, or as a repetitive and trance-inducing device. A cord is knotted each time a verbal spell is spoken. Sometimes the knot will be by itself; at other times, you can tie an object such as a feather, thorn, stick, or even herbs or other objects depending on its aim. For the following witch's ladder, I use slips of willow for a healing spell.

---

[44]. There are many versions of this spell out there; I think it goes back a long way but can't be sure. This one I've adapted myself from several versions in my journals, improvising when needed.

Practicum
Healing Witch's Ladder

Take red cord and nine slips of willow. If you have nine white feathers to weave in as well, all the better. As you knot the cord nine times with the willow sticks, say:

> *By knot of one the spell has begun, healing and wholeness returns*
> *By knot of two it is true, healing and wholeness returns*
> *By knot of three so it shall be, healing and wholeness returns*
> *By knot of four the open door, healing and wholeness returns*
> *By knot of five this spell shall thrive, healing and wholeness returns*
> *By knot of six this spell is fix, healing and wholeness returns,*
> *By knot of seven the stars of heaven, healing and wholeness returns*
> *By knot of eight this spell is fate, healing and wholeness returns*
> *By knot of nine this spell is fine, healing and wholeness returns!*[45]

Store the cord somewhere safe where it will not be disturbed. After it has worked and the person has recovered, take it to the earth to slowly biodegrade.

---

45. Knot spells and rhymes often follow this pattern with numerous variations. I adapt and create mine according to their purpose, as shown here.

Chapter 12
Love Spells

While there is a very long tradition of love spells in folk magic—it is one of the things magical workers are always asked for along with healing, curse-breaking, and prosperity magic—there are surely some ethics involved when we consider drawing someone to us or keeping them with magic. As such, I advise the practitioner to think very carefully before using these spells, and to adapt and add protections and caveats that do not seek control over another unless under the direst of circumstances. While it may be acceptable to bind an ex-lover to leave you alone, to bind one to stay with you against their will is not. One of our best protections is to not engage with activity that comes back around to haunt us, making this a prime area where we can avert trouble later if we apply a little wisdom in the present. What follows in this chapter is a selection of a few traditional love spells should the need arise.

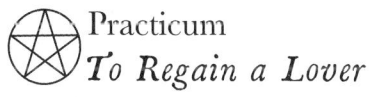

Practicum
To Regain a Lover

First set a good fire, and fast between 11 p.m. and midnight.[46] As midnight strikes, take a small amount of dragon's blood resin and wrap it in fresh white paper. Take it to the fire whilst keeping the name of your love in mind. Set it alight and recite the following:

---
46. This is my adaptation of a traditional West Country spell with a great many variations. Note that it will only work if the lover is willing and hopes to return—it will not work against the will of another.

Dragon's blood, dragons' blood
'Tis not your blood I wish to burn
But my true love's heart I wish to turn
If true loves bond be twixt them and me
May they return and come back to me

Repeat the spell nine times or as you feel until it is done.

Illustration 12: Valerian and Cloth

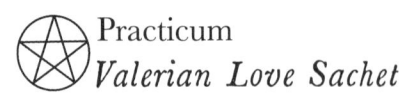

⛤ Practicum
Valerian Love Sachet

This spell is focused on drawing love to the seeker from the right person as yet unknown rather than drawing the love of a specific person. This focus is preferable, as those with poor luck in love often seek it in the wrong places. This spell casts the net wide and makes the person attractive and opens up romantic opportunities.

At a full moon, gather up some valerian flowers when they are in their fullest scent, and beneath the moon wrap them in white cloth, sewing it into a little packet that can be worn around the neck on a cord. Repeat the spell each month while valerian is in flower or has dried until it is effective.

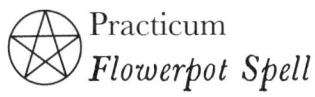

Practicum
Flowerpot Spell

Use this spell to bless a new relationship or call a new positive relationship to you. Take a clean plant pot, compost, and a flower bulb. On a fresh piece of paper, write your love's name upon it, burying it beneath the bulb as you plant it in the pot. Recite the following:

As this flower grows,
So does my love here grow
Towards me and true.

Repeat the charm over and over as you place your hands on the pot and fill it with your energy and blessing. Tend to it and your relationship with equal care.

The general pattern of this spell can be used to grow anything you wish in your life—money, health, a new home—as the plant grows, so shall your new situation.

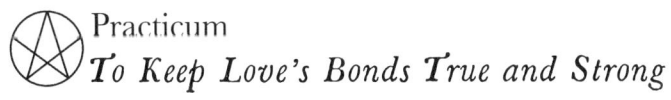

Practicum
To Keep Love's Bonds True and Strong

Under moonlight, take a lock of your hair and of your lover's and plait them together as one, or bind them together with red twine. Repeat three times over three months. Place the hair in a pouch of white cloth, along with dried rose petals and oak leaves, to hang by the bedpost.

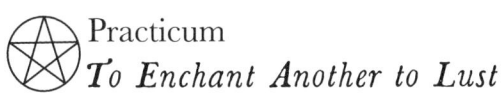

Practicum
To Enchant Another to Lust

In folk magic, goats are often considered unruly, sexual animals, and this spell draws upon the virtues of "Old Horny" to drive a person to lusty desires.

Ethically, I would strongly suggest already having a sexual relationship with the person before performing this spell. Consider it a way to add a little spice and warm things up. Casting this spell on someone who was not consenting would be very unethical and abusive, and it would definitely have awful repercussions, so be warned! As well, be sure to treat the animal ethically—don't harm any animals for this spell. Again, causing harm won't go well for you. This one is for you if and only if you are in a consenting relationship and want to add something a little wild to your time together.

Take the hair from the belly of a goat and tie it into knots while reciting both your names. Hide it in the roof of your lover's house, above their doorway, or over your bed if you live together. When you wish, place the hair in the earth to gently neutralise the magic.

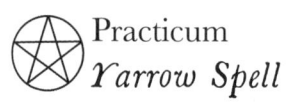

Practicum
Yarrow Spell

This is a very old spell that has many versions and is used to receive a dream or vision of a future partner. What follows is my adaptation. First, find some yarrow growing wild on the grave of a man who died young—the fact that we are working with a plant from a grave hints at much older practices now largely lost but suggests that the magic uses the unspent life force of the person in the grave and that it adds to the spellcaster's own. Above all, never disturb a grave or touch the grave of the recently passed. Instead, seek a very old grave so it remains impersonal and doesn't disturb or disrespect them.

Upon picking the plant, recite:

Yarrow, sweet yarrow
The first that I have found.
In the name of old horny
I pluck you from the ground
As Joseph loved Mary
And took her for his dear
So may I dream this night
And my true love appear![47]

---

47. Graham King, "Gardeners Chronicle, 1875," in *The British Book of Spells and Charms* (Troy Books, 2016), 104.

Practicum
To See One's Future True Love by the Moon

On catching your first glimpse of the new moon, raise your arms and gather in her light to you. Then clasp your hand together tightly in supplication. As you do so, say:

All hail, all hail to thee
All hail to thee, new moon
I pray to thee, new moon
Before thou growest old
To reveal to me
Who my true love shall be[48]

Before the full moon, the supplicant will catch a glimpse of their true love to be.

---

48. Hewett, *Nummits and Crummits*, 71.

Chapter 13
Potions and Powders

Whilst the hearth may be the spirit centre of the home and the garden a place where nature and the wise woman's magic may weave and co-create, there are many magics that need the practical setting of the kitchen for the best results, such as herbal remedies, potions, and other practical items. There is something very down to earth about magic made over the stove or on the kitchen table, and if done consistently, it can become a powerful energy centre in the home, adding its own assistance to the spells and potions made there. This chapter covers various things to make and do in the kitchen, so let's begin by honouring the spirits we may work with there.

A Kitchen Altar

If you have the space, set aside a small space for a kitchen altar—even only a candle and a space to place an offering to the household spirits is enough. In the fairy faith practiced in some places, the tradition is to place a bowl of water for the fairies in the kitchen—this is a good practice to get into along with remembering to ask them for help with any little domestic issues you may have.

Potions and Simmer Pots

Making a simmer pot is easy, but the best ones make use of our connection with plant spirits to add magic to the environment around us in addition to the herbs' scent. The term "simmer pot" as it refers to a magical method is a modern thing, but the practice is as old as making magically infused herbal remedies and using magically charged herbal aromatherapy for its therapeutic effects. Creating these uses all four elements: earth—the botanical plant; water; fire in the heat; and air in the steamy aroma it releases. All elements work together in an excellent example of home-based magic. When we make them with the plant spirits, we can weave unique magical combinations of spirits and materials together for specific magical and environmental effects and use the four elements to release the plant spirits on the steam and scent to work their magic for us wherever we take them.

Practicum
A Winter Blessing Simmer Pot

Use this to fill your home with positive energy and blessing and to create a cosy atmosphere.

Take one litre of fresh spring water (ideally from a spring or charged tap water) and add three sprigs of pine and one slice of lemon. Add a sprig of juniper and few of its berries along with a sprig of rosemary. You may first need to crush your berries and aromatic herbs in a mortar and pestle to aid the release of their fragrant oils. Add a slice or two of fresh ginger or a fresh chopped chilli pepper, and bring gently to a boil, stirring clockwise and visualising sending the fiery rays of the sun into the water. If you like, you may also add three drops of frankincense oil.

After a few minutes, leave to simmer gently until its aromas have filled the space and the brew reduces in volume. Let the steam fill the room. If desired, you can place the heated liquid in appropriate containers on safe surfaces in rooms of the house where it can evaporate further, such as on wood-burning stovetops or radiators, or a few drops once above a lit candle in an aromatherapy burner.

Practicum
A House-Cleansing Simmer Pot

Use this simmer pot as an aid for energetic cleansing or banishing rituals to rid a space of any unwelcome energies.

Gather one litre of fresh spring water, three sprigs of juniper, a handful of juniper berries, a sprig of garden sage, a small handful of wild mugwort, and a few rowan berries or leaves. To this add three drops of peppermint essential oil and a sprinkle of sea salt. Caution: Do not use mugwort if you are pregnant or have menstrual issues.

Gently bring the pot to a boil, stirring slowly in an anticlockwise pattern and asking the herbs to clear and cleanse the space around you and remove any negative energies that may surround you. Let the steam and smell of the pot reach every area of the home.

The mixture can also be strained and added to eco-safe cleaning products to add extra magic when cleaning, especially boundary places like doors and windows.

After a few minutes, leave to simmer gently until the aromas have filled the space and the brew is reduced in volume by evaporation.

Practicum
An Illness-Beating Simmer Pot

Make this simmer pot to fill the air with healing and antiviral and immunity boosting scents and virtues.

To one litre of fresh spring water add a handful of fresh or dried elderberries, a slice of ginger, a slice of lemon, and a handful of rosehips. Add some cinnamon and cloves if you wish.

Bring the mixture to a gentle boil and stir clockwise, seeing the herbs infuse the potion with healing energy. You might like to add a chant to help infuse the brew with your intentions. Try this or make your own:

Healing be thine; wellness be here, healing be thine, wellness be here,
may all illness disappear.

Repeat until you feel the brew's power is suitably potent and the aroma and power of the herbs have filled the space and the brew is reduced in volume by evaporation. This brew can also be consumed as a hot healing drink. Strain and add honey to taste.

⛤ Practicum
A Calming and Dreaming Simmer Pot

This simmer pot can be used to bring an air of peace and tranquillity to a space and aid in a good night's sleep and good dreams. It is ideal to use after any upsetting or traumatic event or after an argument.

To one litre of fresh spring water, add a small handful of lavender flowers, a small sprig of mugwort, a handful of dried or fresh vervain, a small handful of dried hops, and a small handful of chamomile flowers. Last, add three drops each of lavender oil and chamomile oil. Caution: Do not use mugwort if you are pregnant or have menstrual issues.

Bring gently to a boil, stirring slowly clockwise. As you do so, ask the herbs to send calming and supportive energies into the brew. You might like to add your own charging prayers into the water. Here's one example:

Peace be here, rest be here, sweet dreams be here.

Repeat until you feel the brew is fully charged and the scent and thus the plant spirits have filled the whole space.

After a few minutes, leave to simmer gently until its aromas have filled the space and the brew is reduced in volume by evaporation.

⛤ Practicum
Love Potion Simmer Pot

Make this simmer pot potion to increase the home's loving energies and create an air of romance and sensuality.

Start with one litre of fresh spring water or charged tap water—moon water also works well. Add a handful of the most fragrant dried rose petals you can find, a cinnamon stick, the peel of an orange, and a small sprinkle of cayenne. You may wish to crush the orange peel in a mortar and pestle first. To this, add a small handful of meadowsweet and a large spoonful of runny honey. Optionally, you may add three drops of rose essential oil.

As you add each ingredient, speak to it and ask it to assist you. Be clear on what you want it to help you with and what you aim to achieve.

Bring the mixture to a gentle boil, stirring in a clockwise direction. If it is specifically romance you wish to call in, draw a five-pointed pentagram into the water. As you stir, speak a simple chant, such as "Love be here, passion be here, love be here," singing gently to the potion. Drawing up energy from the earth through your arm, charge the brew and see in your inner vision a wave of loving energy rising up in the steam that fills the space.

After a few minutes, leave the mixture to simmer gently until its aromas have filled the space and the brew is reduced in volume by evaporation.

Practicum
Prosperity Simmer Pot

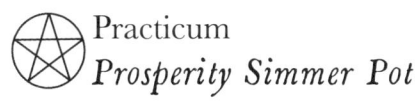

Make this simmer pot to draw in prosperity into your home; it can also be the basis of a space spray to spray around yourself and your wallet to draw in prosperity too.

Take 1 litre of fresh spring or charged tap water, and in a mortar crush with a pestle a teaspoon each of basil, bay leaf, orange peel, and cinnamon, in addition to a single oak leaf. Thank each plant and ask it to assist you in drawing prosperity into your life. Add them to the water and bring to a boil, stirring clockwise, drawing energy up from the earth and into your arm and spoon as you stir and infuse the water with the earth's vast abundance. In your inner vision, see the stirring create a spinning golden spiral that winds inwards, attracting wealth towards you. Let the steam rise and fill the space with prosperity and abundance.

After a few minutes, leave the mixture to simmer gently until its aromas have filled the space and the brew is reduced in volume by evaporation.

When the brew is fully cooled you could add some frankincense essential oil and vibrational essences along with alcohol to make your own prosperity spray to scent the air.

Homemade Protection Sprays

Smoke from incense and herb bundles is the traditional choice for cleansing a home's energies (and is my preference), but it can cause problems—not everywhere is suitable for smoke cleansing, and many homes, especially with children and pets, need to be smoke-free. At other times, we need to clear the energy of the space in a subtler way, such as in public spaces and hospital rooms, as well as around vulnerable people. One modern solution is to make sprays that, similar to simmer pots, have a perfectly valid magical basis—which is a great thing. The thing about folk magic is that it is for the people—the folk! We keep traditions because they serve us just as we allow for change and updates, again because they serve *us*. I therefore consider space sprays as a perfectly valid and useful part of personal magical practice, and there are all sorts of ways we can make them more effective and tailored to our needs.

Practicum
Space-Clearing Protection Spray

You will need

- Water: fresh spring water or distilled water
- Witch hazel astringent or a high ABV percentage vodka or gin
- One or two of the following herbs of your choice: garden sage, mugwort, cedar, juniper leaves and/or berries, rowan berries, St. John's wort
- Prepared flower or energetic essences

Optional

- Sea salt
- Essential oils
- Glass bottle with spray attachment and label

Optional

- Sigils or symbols for further empowerment

Boil the water in a pan with a sprig or two of your chosen herbs. As you place your herbs in the pot, thank their spirits and ask for their assistance to empower your brew, singing and talking to the herbs whilst focusing on your intention. Caution: If you are pregnant or have any menstrual problems, avoid mugwort and only use under the guidance of a professional herbalist.

Let the herbs boil for 10 minutes, stirring clockwise as you charge and bless your work. I like to send energy up from the earth into the pot through my hands and down the wooden spoon into the water. Sometimes I also draw a sigil in the water with the wooden spoon—I allow this to be a very organic process, aiming primarily to be in relationship with the water, the stove's fire, and the herb and plant spirits rather than precisely following a spell or formula. After the mixture begins to boil, let the brew steep until the water has cooled. At this point, add the optional ingredients: sea salt, essential oils, or vibrational essences. If added before the boil, these will evaporate, and we want them to stay in the mixture.

Once completely cooled, strain the mixture and fill a clean dark glass bottle halfway with the brew and top off with the alcohol or witch hazel.

Label the mixture carefully, adding any sigils if you'd like. If stored in a cool, dark place, the spray should last a couple of months.

Note: If you use witch hazel, its smell may overpower the smell of other herbs and oils. It's easier to adjust your mix accordingly with extra essential oil in varieties that complement its scent, such as tea tree, lemon, bergamot, and frankincense.

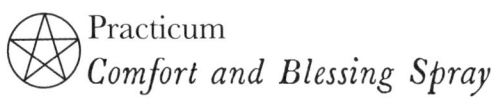

Practicum
Comfort and Blessing Spray

You will need

- Homemade moon water
- Witch hazel or high ABV vodka or gin
- The following herbs (or of your choice): lavender, chamomile, vervain, lemon balm, St. John's wort
- Glass bottle with spray attachment and label

Optional

- Essential oils: frankincense, neroli, sandalwood
- Prepared flower or vibrational essences
- Sigils or symbols for further empowerment

Boil your chosen herbs in the water, asking each herb to bless and charge your work and keep your specific aim in mind. Stir the water slowly, in a clockwise spiral pattern, chanting "All is well, peace be here, all is well, blessings be here" as the brew gradually comes to a boil. Let it boil for 10 minutes or so before letting the potion cool fully and adding any essential oils or vibrational essences.

Strain the mixture and fill a clean dark glass bottle halfway with the brew. Top it off with alcohol or witch hazel.

Label carefully, adding any sigils you may wish to the bottle. If stored in a cool, dark place, the spray should last a couple of months.

Herbal Potions

As well as simmer pots and sprays, there are more traditional ways to work magic in the kitchen, such as making magical oils and herbal tisanes. Here are just a few that may be useful.

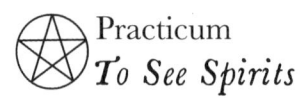

Practicum
To See Spirits

A traditional potion for seeing spirits is to take the leaves of vervain and St. John's wort and crush them to extract the juice with a little spring water drawn from an "eye well"—a well for blessing and healing the vision is all the better, if possible.

Anoint your eyelids with this for three days in a row from the new moon.

Caution: Do not use St. John's wort if you are photosensitive or taking antidepressants or oral contraception.

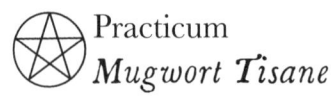

Practicum
Mugwort Tisane

I recommend this brew often—mugwort is excellent for increasing psychic vision and for clearing and consecrating. It is highly protective, making it especially useful for psychic vision helping us to navigate what we see.

Fresh mugwort is best, in which case a few fresh leaves steeped in freshly boiled water for five minutes is enough. Otherwise, use 1 teaspoon of the dried herb to one cup of boiled water. Remember to thank the plant spirit as you work with it. Water from a healthy spring is best, as its lively spirit will also assist you.

Caution: Do not use mugwort if you are pregnant or have menstrual issues.

Practicum
Mugwort Oil

With the plant's blessing, take leaves of mugwort and pack them into a jar. Cover the herbs with vegetable or olive oil and seal tightly. Leave it to steep on a sunny windowsill for at least one month before straining and storing in a cool, dark place.

Mugwort oil may be used to anoint candles or charge and consecrate magical objects. Anoint your eyelids with mugwort oil before divination or visionary practices to assist in deepening and clarifying your vision and insights.

Caution: Do not use mugwort if you have menstrual issues or are pregnant.

Practicum
Elderflower Tisane

Elderflower tisane is excellent for fevers and colds and tastes delicious. It is also a good offering for the spirits. Take 2 teaspoons of the dried herb or a handful of fresh, and steep in hot water for 5 minutes. Add honey or fresh lemon to taste.

Practicum
Ancestral Honouring Oil

- 1 part each
  - Meadowsweet
  - Hawthorn leaves
  - Rosemary
- Dark glass bottle and label

Optional

- 1 part dried aspen leaves

Illustration 13: Ancestral Honouring Oil and Ingredients Around It

Steep the herbs in a bottle of good quality vegetable oil. I like to place my magical oils in the light of the full moon and let them steep in a dark place for a whole lunar month before storing them in a cool, dark cupboard. However, the herbs will become more active if you place the oil on a sunny windowsill for a week first. After one month, strain carefully and store in a dark glass bottle. Remember to label carefully and date. It should be good for a year if kept in a cool, dark place.

Magical Boundary Wash

I like to make a boundary wash for doors and windows or to clean items I sense have bad energy connected to them. The method of making it and its ingredients depend on the circumstances and what I'm washing—some things can't get wet, others may be affected by colour run, and so on—practicalities must come first. This basic recipe for a boundary wash works well most of the time; I use it regularly to wash my doors and gate at key times of the year.

Practicum
Boundary Wash Recipe

- 1 cup fresh soapwort (or ½ cup dried)
- 1 tablespoon sea salt
- 1 tablespoon juniper
- 1 litre hot water

Optional

- Rowan stick
- Florida water soap

Ideally, use fresh spring water gathered from a local well, but tap water will do. I like to heat the water in a pan over a fire to add the fire energy and the living water energy from the holy water I draw the water from into the potion; I am lucky and can do this easily in my garden but haven't always had this much space. In those times, I made this in the kitchen over an electric stove!

Slowly bring the water to a boil and add the soapwort, salt, and juniper, thanking each as they are added, stirring to add the wash's intent. My favourite thing to stir with is a rowan stick, but I've also used a wooden kitchen spoon—use what you have to hand. After doing some experimentation, I've enjoyed using Florida water soap in this recipe; if that feels right to you, shave off some soap from the bar and add it. Your intuition and whatever's growing around you should be your first point of guidance. After adding whatever you wish to the mixture, wait until the salt has dissolved and set it aside until it is cool enough to use.

You can add this wash to conventional cleaning products or use it on its own to wash your front door and anywhere else it is needed. If using on windows, you may need extra time to rinse afterward—again, use common sense and adapt to meet your personal needs.

Practicum
Banishing Powder

This powder works well for banishing unwanted energies from your home in the form of bad neighbours, bad habits, unwelcome spirits, and malicious magic. The powder can be used in many ways. Wrap an item from the unwanted person with the powder and keep in a secret place until they have left, sprinkle some powder at the home's gateway of a troublesome neighbour, draw a circle of powder around a black candle to banish someone's malicious magic or ill will, and so on. Bowls of banishing powder can also be placed around a home if it has severe negative energy or malicious ghosts. The powder can be steeped in oil and used to draw an X on a photo or on the offender's personal items.

You will need

- Dried garlic granules or powder (garlic salt is also acceptable)
- Sea salt
- Hearth ashes (you could also substitute black salt [recipe on following page] or herbal black salt according to your preferences)
- Ochre (If you can't find it, red brick dust can be used as substitute.)
- Peppercorns
- Blackthorn leaves
- Glass jar and label

The proportions of this recipe can vary depending on your intuition and what's on hand, but equal parts of all ingredients is a good place to start. Crush all the ingredients together with a mortar and pestle, speaking as you do so to imbue them with your will. Thank each ingredient and tell it that it will be used to banish all ill will and negative magics. You may like to place your hands over the mixture to send it this intention and charge it up or even place it on your altar for a while. When you feel it is duly charged energetically, store it in a clean glass jar, labelled with ingredients and the date of creation. Make a fresh jar of this once a year, as older powder may lose its potency.

Witch's Black Salt

Whilst the term "black salt" can refer to Himalayan black salt or the kiln-fired rock salt used in Indian cuisine and some witchcraft practices, it also describes something made specifically for magic used for banishing, cursing, binding, and cleansing. Its roots are in American hoodoo magic, where the individual ingredients are used for the same purposes in European magic, an example of a practice I personally have no problem adapting to my use. Here I use the name for ease of understanding.

This recipe can also vary depending on circumstances and your intuition. For example, I use magical ashes from my Samhain or Bealtaine fire or from burnt blackthorn and juniper. Whatever you include think about it carefully and be clear on the why of each decision.

Practicum
Black Salt

You will need

- Equal parts
    - Sea salt
    - Magical ashes (I prefer blackthorn and juniper)
    - Powdered eggshells
    - Peppercorns
- Glass jar and label

Optional

- Iron or rust shavings
- Cayenne pepper
- Dragon's blood

Grind the ingredients together in a mortar with a pestle. Store the powder in a dark glass jar, taking care to label and date it. Charge under a full moon.

Witch's Dragon Powder

Another powerful boundary protector is a powder from dragon's blood, brick dust, and cayenne pepper crushed together in a mortar with a pestle that is sprinkled at the house's boundary lines. It can also be sprinkled over things requiring protection and over people during any banishing ritual.

Note the colour red and the fiery attributes of these ingredients—this is an example of sympathetic magic, this one of protection with the element of fire.

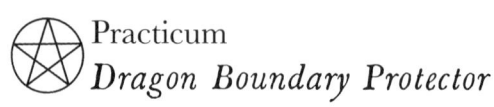

Practicum
Dragon Boundary Protector

You will need

- Equal parts
  - Dragon's blood
  - Brick dust
  - Cayenne pepper*
- Jar for storage and label

* If cayenne and brick dust are unsuitable for use for any reason, substitute with rosemary and rowan berries.

Crush and stir the powders together. Drawing energy up from the earth, push power into the powder as you crush the ingredients together. You may also like to place your hands over it and charge it that way. Here's an additional verbal charm to be spoken over it:

Dragon's fire, blood fire, boundary holder, I charge you to let no ill will pass you, and to repel all unwelcome spirits!

Repeat as necessary. Take care to renew the charge at least once a year, ideally at Samhain or during the early winter before the long nights take hold.

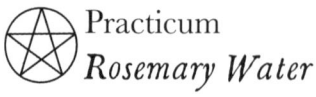

Practicum
Rosemary Water

For a quick remedy that transforms the atmosphere in a home and casts away stuck or negative energy, create a wash or simmer pot of rosemary boiled in fresh spring water for 30 minutes until its scent fills the space. Add a little sea salt to the wash for extra potency in clearing away stuck energy or staleness and to ground upset feelings. This is especially effective after arguments, illness, or bad dreams.

Boil the rosemary over a low simmering heat for as long as you wish to have the home filled with its aroma. When the water has cooled, you may use it to wash the doors windows, gates, or boundaries. Take care to wash door handles with it and pour onto outside doormats or front steps.

Incense and Herb Bundle Recipes

Burning herbs or incenses is a useful part of magic that is easy to do and can serve as a powerful offering to the spirits. It is a huge subject, too large to cover in its entirety in this book. What follows are a few simple recipes to try or get you started.

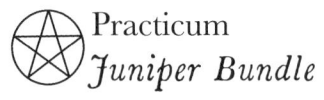

Practicum
Juniper Bundle

Juniper is an excellent herb for saining and glanadh, the ritual cleaning of a space. Preparing a juniper or other herb bundle is easy if you can find sprigs of fresh juniper.

Lay your lengths of fresh juniper, around five or six inches on a piece of newspaper. Place this upon your thigh and roll back and forth so that you are rolling the herb into a tighter and tighter roll. After a few minutes, tie tightly, up and down the length of the herb in a criss cross pattern to keep it all in one shape. Tie it tighter than you think it'll need so that it holds when it has dried and shrunk a little. Hang your herb bundle in an airy place such as in the window to dry fully before use.

In addition to juniper, you can use this same method with rosemary, lavender, garden sage, cedar, and any other herbs or suitable aromatic trees. Combinations of juniper and rosemary or juniper and lavender work particularly well.

⛤ Practicum
Protection Incense

This powdered incense will need to be burnt on a charcoal brick in a suitable container.

- 3 parts frankincense
- 1 part sandalwood
- 2 parts dragon's blood
- 1 part dried rowan
- 1 part dried rosemary
- 1 part juniper berries

Combine all parts in a mortar. With a pestle, crush and imbue the mixture with your intention, thanking each ingredient for its assistance as it is added.

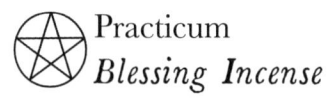

⛤ Practicum
Blessing Incense

This powdered incense will need to burn on a charcoal brick in a suitable container.

- 3 parts frankincense
- 2 parts ash leaves
- 3 parts dried vervain
- 1 part benzoin

Combine all parts in a mortar. With a pestle, crush and imbue with your intention, thanking each ingredient for its assistance as you add it.

Practicum
Offering Incense

This powdered incense needs to burn on a charcoal brick in a suitable container.

- 4 parts frankincense
- 2 parts sandalwood
- 1 part rose petals
- 1 part hawthorn leaves
- 2 parts vervain

Combine all parts in a mortar. With a pestle, crush and imbue with your intention, thanking each ingredient for its assistance as you add it.

Conclusion

I hope you have found some ways in these pages to develop and unfold your own wild witchcraft and folk magic practice. Each of us has a unique position on this ancient and winding path, each with its own gifts and challenges. May you find things here that help you, things learned by those who have gone before or walk alongside you to be added to what you've found to make your magic wild and wise and your hearthfire glow with blessings, health, and abundance. We all have the right to be here and form connection to the deep, wild currents of the land—all we need to do is but reach out. We each can draw from the well of the craft and drink of its waters and, together, with our stories, spirit kin, crafts, and skills, make from it our own unique brew. May yours be rich and heady!

Dear ones, I ask you to be wise and kind. With clear eyes, look at your hearts and magic to see your place in the world. May each step you take bring blessedness and serve life and the ancient ones who oversee our work. May you find yourself one day at one with the land, your heart full, eyes full of laughter, and hands to hold the soul of the world that let it fly free like a blackbird at dawn. And when the time comes, may you sit at the hearth with the best of us beyond the fields we know, whispering in the ears of young ones yet to be born as they make their way out upon the paths in springs and summers yet to come.

Appendix
Planetary Virtues, Sigils, and Other Symbols

The seven classical planets—the moon, sun, Mars, Mercury, Jupiter, Venus, and Saturn—have been important to Western magic at least since the days of ancient Mesopotamia. Called wandering stars, they were known in ancient Greece to correspond with the days of the week, lending their astronomical virtues to the qualities of each passage of time, punctuating the rhythms of each day, week, and year. Each of these planets has traditional areas of rulership and influence as well as a host of correspondences: colours, herbs, incenses, ruling angels, and many more.

Planetary magic can be added to your practice or serve as a point of deep exploration, a subject all its own. Both this and astrology were a favourite of British cunning folk in times past, and they observed that the planets' powers could influence even the smallest details of our lives. For centuries, contact with these forces benefitted practitioners in many ways, allowing them to align with their energies and enlist them for support, culminating in a huge body of tradition and practical lore from which we still draw today.

For our purposes here, I include a short, basic guide to the planets and planetary sigils for use in all the spells and practica should you wish to include them. They are particularly useful when inscribed into candles for spellwork when aligned with the correct day, for example. When relevant, including a relevant planetary sigil on written spells or the labels of potions or other magical containers can add extra potency. Again, performing magic with the ruling planet in mind as well as the season and lunar phase can help us work in alignment with the greater forces of creation and lend power and potency to our work.

Moon (Monday)

The moon occupies a special position in many people's hearts in addition to magical practitioners; she is often referred to as the queen of heaven. Although many traditions around the world believe the moon to be masculine in nature, most in our traditions consider the moon to be a female presence or expressing a feminine energy, and there are a great many lunar goddesses historically worshipped across Europe. The influence of the moon upon women's reproductive cycles has been long known and widely observed, as are its effects upon mental health and our emotions. The moon also influences the tides. The moon is good for magic related to water, healing, dreams, divination, intuition, and contacting the dead. Its subtle, shifting silvery presence helps us align and understand the nature of things unseen that defy linear logic and solid definitions. It emanates energies of nuance and liminality, hence its special place in the hearts of witches and magicians the world over.

Mars (Tuesday)

Fiery and battle ready, Mars was also the name of the Roman god of war, known as Ares to the ancient Greeks. Forwards moving, aggressive, passionate Mars rules over warriors and the righteous, offering protection to those in need as well as overseeing bloodshed and destruction. Mars also has rulership of other martial pursuits such as competitiveness, sports, ambitions, radical change, pride, prowess, vigour, masculine virtues, and sexuality. It is fiery, bold, shiny, and youthful.

Mercury (Wednesday)

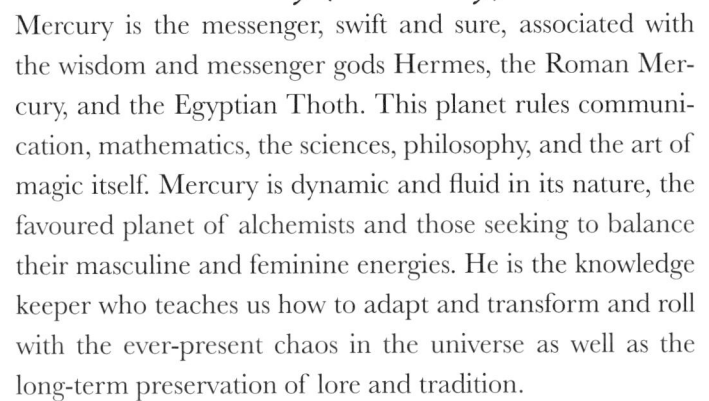

Mercury is the messenger, swift and sure, associated with the wisdom and messenger gods Hermes, the Roman Mercury, and the Egyptian Thoth. This planet rules communication, mathematics, the sciences, philosophy, and the art of magic itself. Mercury is dynamic and fluid in its nature, the favoured planet of alchemists and those seeking to balance their masculine and feminine energies. He is the knowledge keeper who teaches us how to adapt and transform and roll with the ever-present chaos in the universe as well as the long-term preservation of lore and tradition.

Jupiter (Thursday)

Expansive Jupiter is the key planet to work with for wealth, generosity, exuberance. Jupiter is sometimes described as the "all-parent" who cares for others with his largesse and benevolence. Jupiter is also a planet of purification, healing, and the regal qualities of honourable conduct and rising above base behaviour. Sometimes called on for love magic, Jupiter is also helpful for virility magic, tact, and persuasiveness, as well as abundance of all kinds—affection, humour, camaraderie, and charm.

Venus (Friday)

Venus is the bringer of beauty, love, sensuality, and kindness. Art and hedonistic pleasures are all under Venus's rule, as are crafts and the craftiness to get what you desire. Teaching the power and potential of physical embodiment of the spirit, she shows us that we are infinite beings incarnated on a material plane in a material body and shows us the joys of the flesh as a route to magical power and ascension. In addition to being useful for love spells, Venus can heal relationships of all kinds including our relationship with ourselves and our own bodies and humanity. Glamour, reflective magic, and spiritual ecstasy are all Venus related.

Saturn (Saturday)

The eldest and "old man" of the planets, Saturn is said to be bound in chains by the Romans. Saturn rules over constriction, death, decrease, and decay. Yet from it springs new life and Saturn teaches when it is time to let the old die so that the new may live. In being the keeper of our sorrows and shadows, Saturn rules over what we resist and deny, yet he also shows us the value of boundaries, preservation, and rules, as well as silence and solitude. The planet of scholars and the keeper of time itself, Saturn's power touches us all. In doing so, we learn the deep work of the soul.

Sun (Sunday)

The *Sol Invictus*, "unconquered sun" as it was known in Rome, is the centre of our solar system and as such rules over sovereignty, healing, success, cleansing and clarity, wealth, luck and victory. As the leader of our days, the sun shows us the power in the great cycles of the day and the year, from night to day, from the winter solstice to the summer solstice and back again. The sun also is the great guide to our soul's journey through the underworld, just as it was believed to do every night in cultures around the world. The guide and mercy of the dead, bringing life after death, renewal, and regeneration. The sun as teacher and leader becomes our ultimate path to our spiritual growth.

Other Useful Symbols for Magic

Sigils and symbols comprise a vast branch of magic unto themselves, so I'll not go too far here as there are plenty of resources out there. What follows are some classic symbols in addition to planetary sigils that can be used for common magical aims. Like the planetary sigils, these symbols can be inscribed on candles, drawn in written spells, and even drawn in herbs, salt, or blessed liquids on suitable surfaces. The symbols can also be painted onto objects, depending on your purposes.

Arrow: For victory and assertive aims.

Currency symbols (£/$/€): Using the symbols for money specific to your location are excellent for money and prosperity magic.

Eye: The all-seeing eye is an excellent protection symbol.

Hearts: For love spells including friendship and family love.

Pentagram: A five-pointed star is often used to charge items and generally imbue something with power.

Spiral or Triple spiral: I use spirals for offerings and prayers to honour spirits and the flow of life.

X: Cross for banishing and denying power to someone or something.

Bibliography

Print

Carmichael, Alexander. *Carmina Gadelica: Hymns and Incantations*. Floris Books, 1994. Originally published 1900 by Oliver & Boyd.

Chambers, Ian. *The Witch Compass: Working with the Winds in Traditional Witchcraft*. Llewellyn Publications, 2022.

Chambers, Robert. *Popular Rhymes of Scotland*. W&R Chambers, 1870.

David, Ross, and Gavin D. Smith. *Scots-English/English-Scots Dictionary*. Hippocrene Practical Dictionary, 1998.

Davies, Owen. *Grimoires: A History of Magic Books*. OUP Oxford, 2010.

Davies, Owen. *A People Bewitched: Witchcraft and Magic in Nineteenth-Century Somerset*. FW Media, 2012.

Davies, Owen. *Popular Magic: Cunning folk in English History*. Hambledon Continuum, 2007.

Dowd, Marion. "Bewitched by an Elf Dart: Fairy Archaeology, Folk Magic and Traditional Medicine in Ireland." In *Cambridge Archaeological Journal* 28, no. 3 (2018): 451–73.

Evans-Wentz, W. Y. *The Fairy Faith in Celtic Countries*. Dover Publications, 2002.

Forest, Danú. *Celtic Tree Magic: Ogham Lore and Druid Mysteries*. Llewellyn Publications, 2014.

Forest, Danú. *Gwyn ap Nudd, Wild God of Faerie, Guardian of Annfwn*. Moon Books, 2017.

Forest, Danú. *The Magical Year: Seasonal Celebrations to Honor Nature's Ever-Turning Wheel*. Watkins, 2016.

Forest, Danú. *Wild Magic: Celtic Folk Traditions for the Solitary Practitioner*. Llewellyn Publications, 2020.

Forest, Danú, and Dan Goodfellow. *Celtic Goddesses, Witches and Queens*. Schiffer, 2023.

Garry, Gemma. *The Black Toad: West Country Witchcraft and Magic*. Troy Books, 2011.

Garry, Gemma. *Traditional Witchcraft: A Cornish Book of Ways*. Troy Books, 2008.

Haddon, Alfred Cort. *The Study of Man*. G.P. Putnam's Sons, 1898.

Halliwell-Phillipps, James. "IX–Superstition–Rhymes." In *Popular Rhymes and Nursery Tales (1820–89)*, 46. Accessed June 7, 2024. https://www.gutenberg.org/cache/epub/35707/pg35707-images.html#ix-superstition-rhymes.

Harland, John. *Lancashire Folklore*. Frederick Warne & Co, 1882, 62. Online edition from Project Gutenberg. Accessed June 7, 2024. https://www.gutenberg.org/files/41148/41148-h/41148-h.htm#Page_62.

Harms, Daniel. *Witch Bottles: History, Culture, Magic*. Avalonia Books, 2022.

Henderson, Lizanne, and Edward J. Cowan. *Scottish Fairy Belief*. Tuckwell Press, 2001.

Hewett, Sarah. *Nummits and Crummits: Devonshire Customs, Characteristics and Folk-Lore*. Forgotten Books, 2020. Originally published 1900 by Thomas Burleigh.

Hoggard, Brian, *Magical House Protection: The Archaeology of Counter-Witchcraft*. Berghann Books, 2021.

Hull, Eleanor, ed. "The Saltair Na Rann attributed to Oenghus the Culdee, 9–10th century" *Poem Book of the Gael*. Browne and Howell, 1913.

Hutton. Ronald. *Stations of the Sun: A History of the Ritual Year in Britain.* Oxford University Press, 2001.

Hutton, Ronald. *The Witch: A History of Fear, from Ancient Times to the Present.* Yale University Press, 2017.

Jones, Kelvin. *Seven Cornish Witches.* Oakmagic Publications, 1998.

King, Graham. *The British Book of Charms and Spells.* Troy Books, 2016.

Kinsman, John. *The Cornish Folklore Handbook.* Oakmagic Publications, 1997.

Kirk, Robert. *The Secret Commonwealth of Elves, Fauns, and Fairies.* Dover Books, 2008.

Legard, Phil, and Alexander Cummins. *An Excellent Booke of the Arte of Magicke.* Scarlet Imprint, 2020.

Lenihan, Eddie. *Meeting the Other Crowd: The Fairy Stories of Hidden Ireland.* Gill & Macmillan, 2003.

Lindahl, Carl, John McNamara, and John Lindow. *Medieval Folklore: A Guide to Myths, Legends, Beliefs, and Customs.* Oxford University Press, 2002.

Mac Neill, Máire. *The Festival of Lughnasa: A Study of the Celtic Festival of the Beginning of the Harvest.* University College Dublin, 1982, 10–11.

Patterson, Steve. *Cecil Williamson's Book of Witchcraft: A Grimoire of the Museum of Witchcraft.* Troy Books, 2014.

Pearson, Nigel G. *Treading the Mill: Workings in Traditional Witchcraft.* Troy Books, 2016.

Sharp, Cecil, ed. "Traditional Folk Song." In *Folk Songs from Somerset,* Simpkin & Co., the Wessex Press, 1904. Accessed April 27, 2024. https://archive.org/details/imslp-songs-from-somerset-sharp-cecil/SIBLEY1802.5603.14249.2bee- 39087013594496fifthseries/page/n83/mode/2up?q=somerset.

Sikes, Wirt. *British Goblins: Welsh Folk-Lore, Fairy Mythology, Legends and Traditions.* EP Publishing, 1973. Originally published 1880, Sampson and Low.

Simpson, Jacqueline, and Steve Roud. *Oxford Dictionary of English Folklore.* Oxford University Press, 2003.

Smith, Andrew Phillip. *Pages from a Welsh Cunning Man's Book: Magic and Fairies in Nineteenth-Century Wales.* Bardic Press, 2023.

Suggett, Richard. *A History of Magic and Witchcraft in Wales*. The History Press, 2008.

Suggett, Richard. *Welsh Witches: Narratives of Witchcraft and Magic from Sixteenth- and Seventeenth-Century Wales*. Atramentous Press, 2018.

Thomas, Val. *Of Chalk and Flint: A Way of Norfolk Magic*. Troy Books, 2019.

Trevelyan, Marie. *Welsh Witchcraft Charms and Spells*. Oakmagic Publications, 2012.

Wilby, Emma. *Cunning Folk and Familiar Spirits: Shamanistic Visionary Traditions in Early Modern British Witchcraft and Magic*. Sussex Academic Press, 2013.

Wilby, Emma. *The Visions of Isobel Gowdie: Magic, Witchcraft and Dark Shamanism in Seventeenth-Century Scotland*. Liverpool University Press, 2010.

Young, S. R. *Boggarts, Fairies, and Cunning Men: Some Forgotten Lancashire Folklore Essays*. Pwca, 2023.

Online

"249—Charm: Garlic." Museum of Witchcraft and Magic. Accessed February 27, 2024. https://museumofwitchcraftandmagic.co.uk/object/charm-garlic.

"Biddy Early." Clare Library. Accessed February 28, 2024. https://www.clarelibrary.ie/eolas/coclare/people/biddy.htm.

"Fairy," Online Etymological Dictionary. Accessed February 27, 2024. https://www.etymonline.com/search?q=fairy.

"Fay." Online Etymology Dictionary. Accessed February 27, 2024. https://www.etymonline.com/word/fay#etymonline_v_1175.

"Glan." Foclóir New Irish-English dictionary. Accessed February 27, 2024. https://www.focloir.ie/en/dictionary/ei/glan.

"Rod." Museum of Witchcraft and Magic. Accessed February 27, 2024. https://museumofwitchcraftandmagic.co.uk/object/wand-rod/.

"Somerset Wassail." Hymns and Carols of Christmas. Accessed February 27, 2024. https://www.hymnsandcarolsofchristmas.com/Hymns_and_Carols/somerset_wassail.htm.

"Tam Lin: 39G." Tam Lin Balladry. Accessed February 27, 2024. https://www.tam-lin.org/versions/39G.html.

"Toradh." Teanglann Dictionary and Language Library. Accessed February 27, 2024. https://www.teanglann.ie/en/fgb/toradh.

Index

Airt, 45

ancestor, 6, 27, 29, 152, 157, 172, 173

ash (tree), 42, 60, 91, 98, 101, 102, 143, 194, 218

ash, 98, 99, 183, 214, 215

Bible, 74, 75

Brigit, 7, 17, 26, 27, 73, 92, 93, 96, 110, 152

Bucca, 39, 40, 60, 115

candle, 17, 18, 22, 28–30, 47, 52, 56, 60, 67, 68, 70, 72, 85–87, 89, 91, 92, 115, 125, 159, 162, 169, 177–182, 203, 204, 214

Caim, 41–47, 70, 86, 91, 113, 159, 160, 169

cauldron, 56–58, 121, 124

charm, 16, 18, 19, 61, 62, 83, 94–97, 101, 126–129, 140, 146–148, 156, 187, 188, 191, 193, 199, 216, 225

crossing, 79, 85, 88, 102, 169

compass, 15, 26, 41–45, 99

cunning, 2, 4–6, 8, 13, 15, 31, 32, 37, 51, 58, 59, 63, 64, 66, 68, 69, 77, 81, 117, 143, 155, 156, 163, 164, 175, 223

deisil, 17, 43, 45

Tuatha, 45

staff, 6, 32, 39, 42, 44, 51–55, 112, 143

stang, 13, 44, 51, 52

elder, 77, 132, 135, 144, 186

fire, 2, 6, 8, 11, 18, 20, 26, 42, 46, 55–57, 61, 71, 72, 76, 86–91, 97–99, 107, 110–112, 132, 144, 146, 150, 152, 155, 158, 160, 183, 191, 197, 204, 209, 213, 215, 216

Hag stone, 16, 25, 26, 77, 94, 95, 186
hex, 5, 85, 103, 143
incense, 20, 22, 57–59, 61, 65, 71, 72, 86, 90–92, 113, 136, 138–141, 145, 159, 160, 207, 217–219
moon, 14, 28, 31, 34, 44, 66–68, 70, 83, 97, 98, 100, 101, 107, 117–129, 147, 149, 151, 169, 179, 180, 186, 189, 191, 192, 199, 201, 206, 209, 210, 212, 215, 223, 224
oak, 47, 49, 60, 90, 132, 143, 145, 146, 199, 207
rowan, 16, 18, 19, 60, 90, 95, 98, 146, 194, 205, 208, 213, 216, 218
spring, 1, 2, 11, 20, 46, 57, 61, 65, 67, 83, 91, 99, 107, 110, 111, 113, 121, 141, 149–152, 188, 191, 192, 204–208, 210, 213, 217
water, 10, 11, 19, 20, 32, 36, 42, 46, 55, 57–59, 61, 64–67, 71, 77–79, 83, 84, 86, 89–93, 97, 99, 110, 119, 121, 122, 132, 135, 141, 149–153, 158–161, 167, 188, 189, 191, 192, 203–211, 213, 216, 217, 224

witch, 4–6, 15, 16, 18, 31, 34, 36, 38–40, 58, 59, 69, 83, 84, 90, 99, 100, 102–105, 107, 111, 117, 124, 131, 132, 136, 138, 140, 144, 155, 156, 164, 166, 171, 194, 195, 208–210, 215, 216
willow, 25, 58, 132, 147, 192–195
well, 3, 5, 6, 9–11, 14, 16–19, 24, 29, 32, 33, 35, 36, 38, 40, 44, 45, 47, 52, 55, 57, 58, 60, 61, 63, 66, 68, 71–73, 76, 78, 81, 82, 84, 93, 101–105, 109–113, 117, 123, 124, 131, 135–145, 149, 152, 158, 159, 165–168, 171, 180, 182, 186, 194, 195, 200, 206, 207, 209, 210, 212–214, 217, 221, 223–226

To Write to the Author

If you wish to contact the author or would like more information about this book, please write to the author in care of Llewellyn Worldwide Ltd. and we will forward your request. Both the author and publisher appreciate hearing from you and learning of your enjoyment of this book and how it has helped you. Llewellyn Worldwide Ltd. cannot guarantee that every letter written to the author can be answered, but all will be forwarded. Please write to:

Danu Forest
℅ Llewellyn Worldwide
2143 Wooddale Drive
Woodbury, MN 55125-2989

Please enclose a self-addressed stamped envelope for reply, or $1.00 to cover costs. If outside the U.S.A., enclose an international postal reply coupon.

Many of Llewellyn's authors have websites with additional information and resources. For more information, please visit our website at http://www.llewellyn.com.

Notes